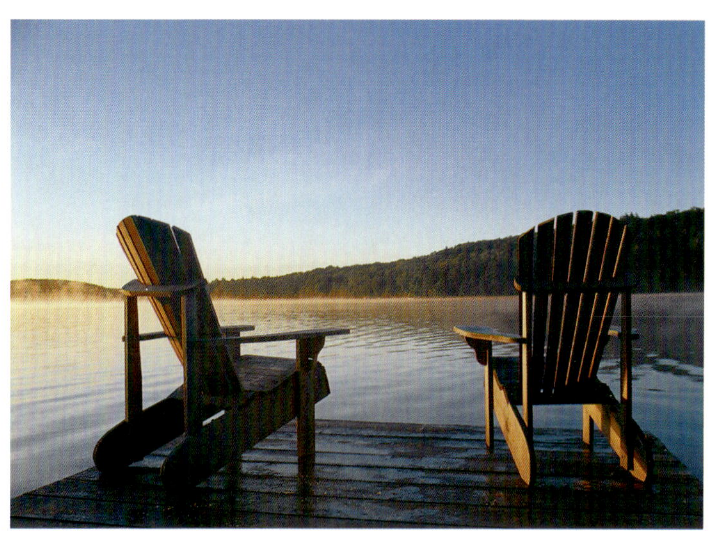

ONTARIO'S COTTAGE COUNTRY

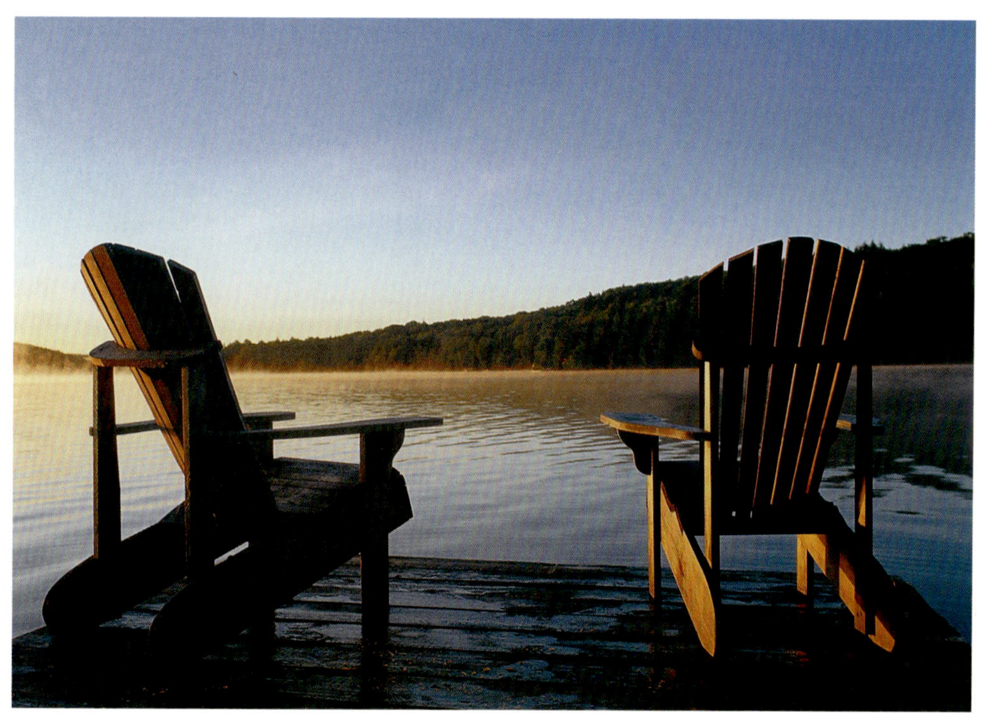

WHITECAP BOOKS
VANCOUVER / TORONTO / NEW YORK

Text by Tanya Lloyd
Edited by Elaine Jones
Photo editing by Tanya Lloyd
Proofread by Lisa Collins
Cover and interior layout by Maxine Lea

Printed and bound in Canada

National Library of Canada Cataloguing in Publication Data

Lloyd, Tanya, 1973–
Ontario's cottage country

(Canada series)
ISBN 1-55285-180-X

1. Muskoka (Ont.)—Pictorial works. I. Title.
FC3095.M88L56 2001 971.3'1604'0222 C2001-910094-9
F1059.M9L56 2001

The publisher acknowledges the support of the Canada Council and the Cultural Services Branch of the Government of British Columbia in making this publication possible. We acknowledge the financial support of the Government of Canada through the Book Publishing Industry Development Program for our publishing activities.

For more information on the Canada Series and other Whitecap Books titles, please visit our web site at www.whitecap.ca.

In Ontario's cottage country, water beckons from every direction—from the churning grey waves of the Great Lakes, from the rippling patterns on Lake Muskoka, and from the swift rivers of Algonquin Park. Here, a retreat from the world is only a short drive, hike, or paddle away.

What an Ontario resident calls a cottage could be a luxury mansion with its own private marina. It could also be a one-room cabin passed from generation to generation since farmers and traders first settled the region. It might lie on the shores of Georgian Bay, in the forests of the Haliburton Highlands, in the Thousand Islands, or along the Rideau River. But whether in the Muskokas or tucked along the Niagara Escarpment, most have a few things in common.

A pair of Muskoka chairs stand on the deck, a perfect place for watching the sunset. A canoe lies ready on the lawn, its dark green hull absorbing the sun. A flagpole marks the front walk and, on the winding road behind, a handmade wooden sign points visitors in the right direction. The details may differ, but most cottagers agree on one thing—there's nothing more relaxing than a sunny day by the water.

Of course, once the fishing gear's packed and the picnic is ready, a cottage isn't actually necessary. All that's really needed is some water. And with 250,000 lakes and rivers, 3,840 kilometres (2,400 miles) of coastline, and 100,000 kilometres (60,000 miles) of river, there is no shortage in Ontario. Whether they're fishing for whitefish and trout or searching for the perfect waterskiing weather, more visitors each year discover the summer paradise known as Ontario's cottage country.

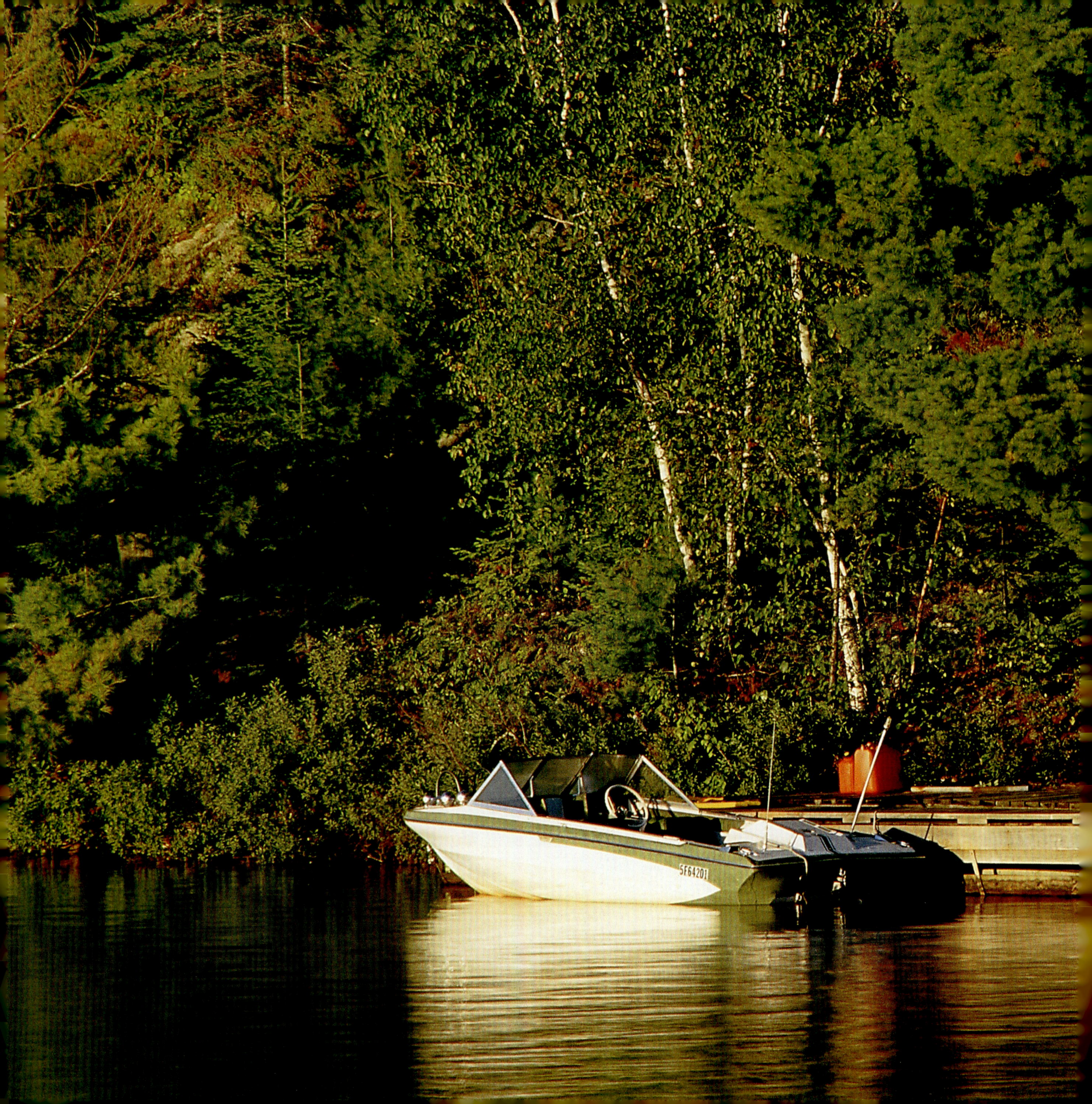
5F64201

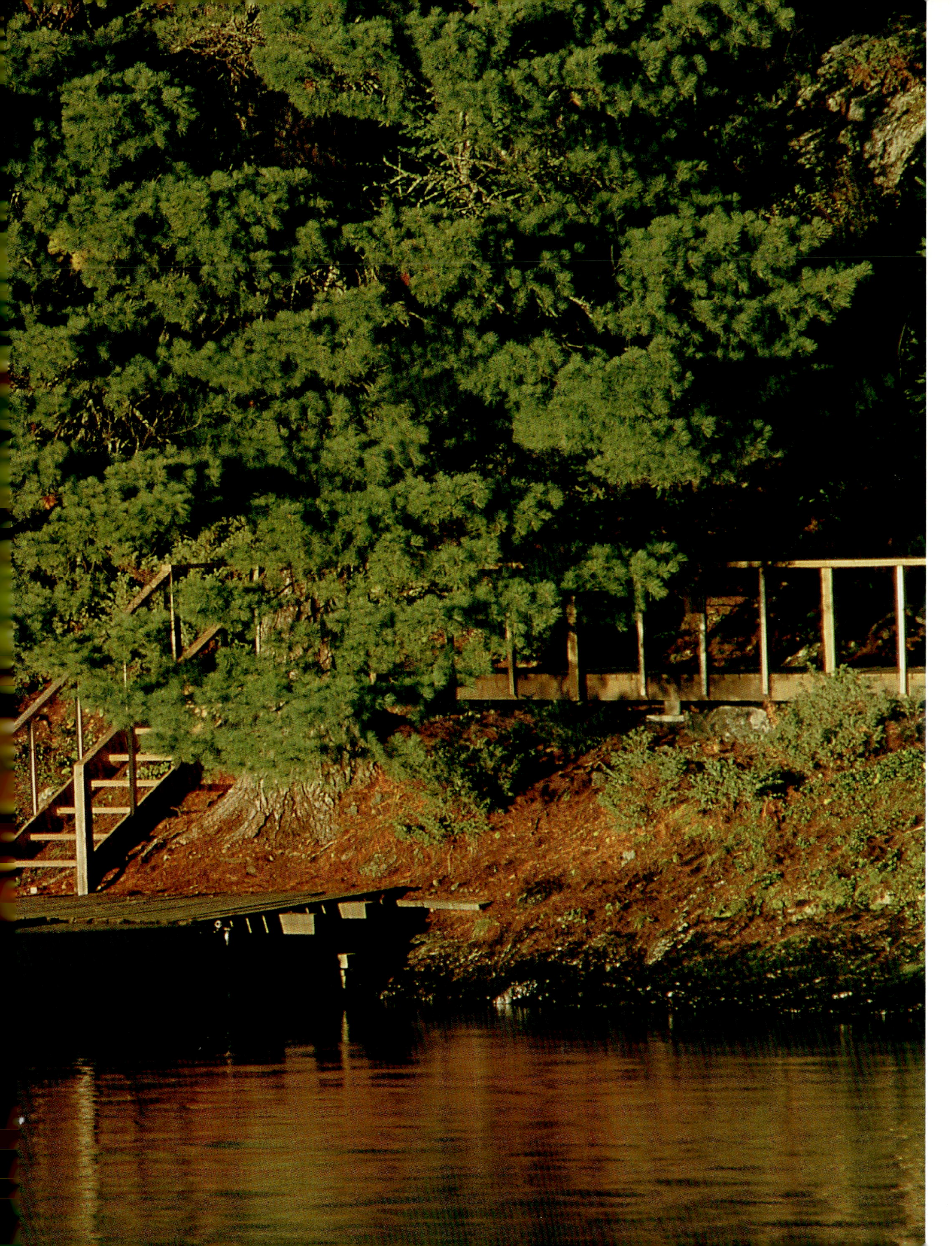

Carved by the glaciers of the last ice age, Lake of the Woods is dotted with more than 14,000 islands. It was called *Minestic*, or Lake of the Islands, by the Ojibwa people who lived here when the first French settlers arrived.

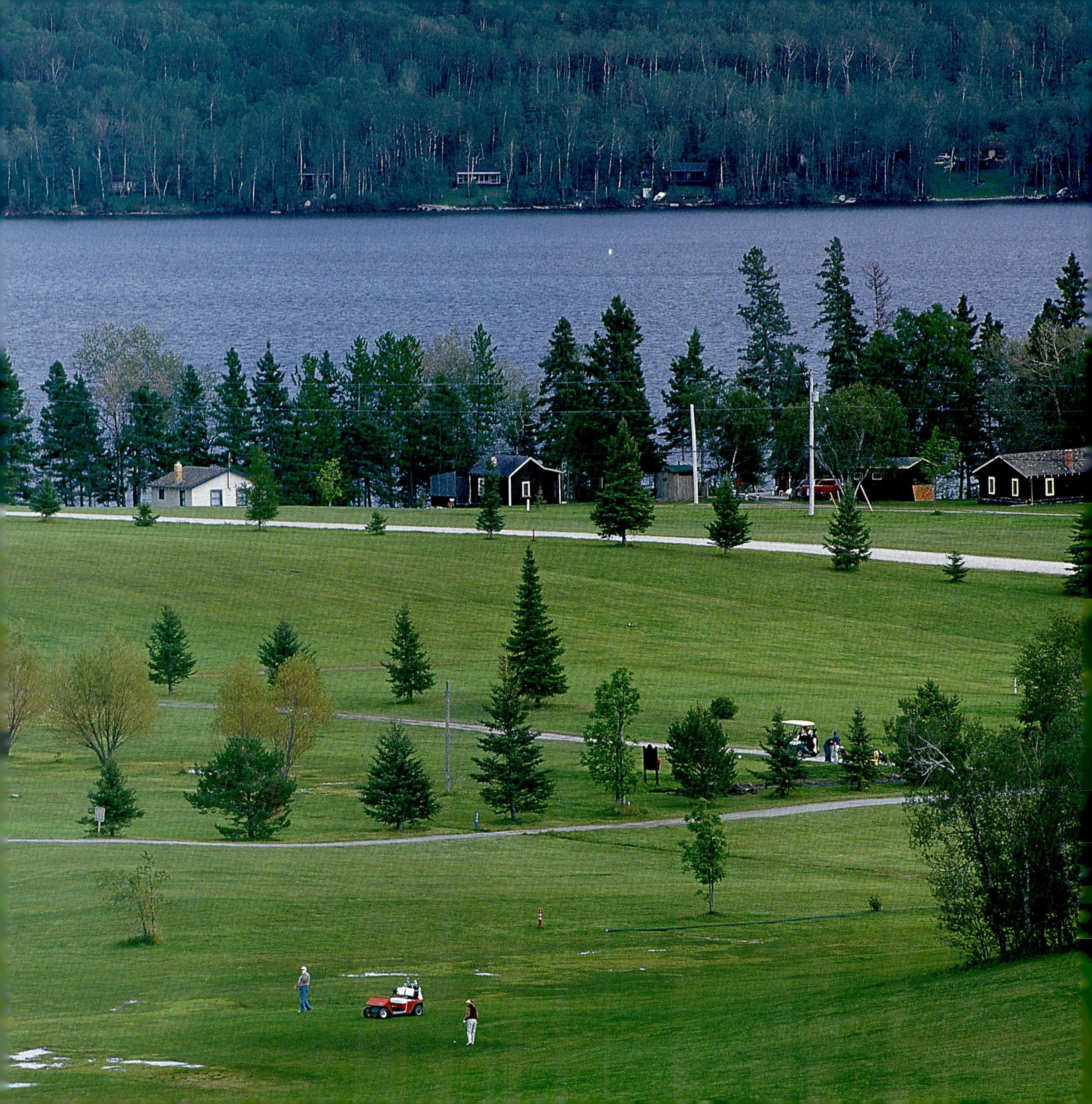

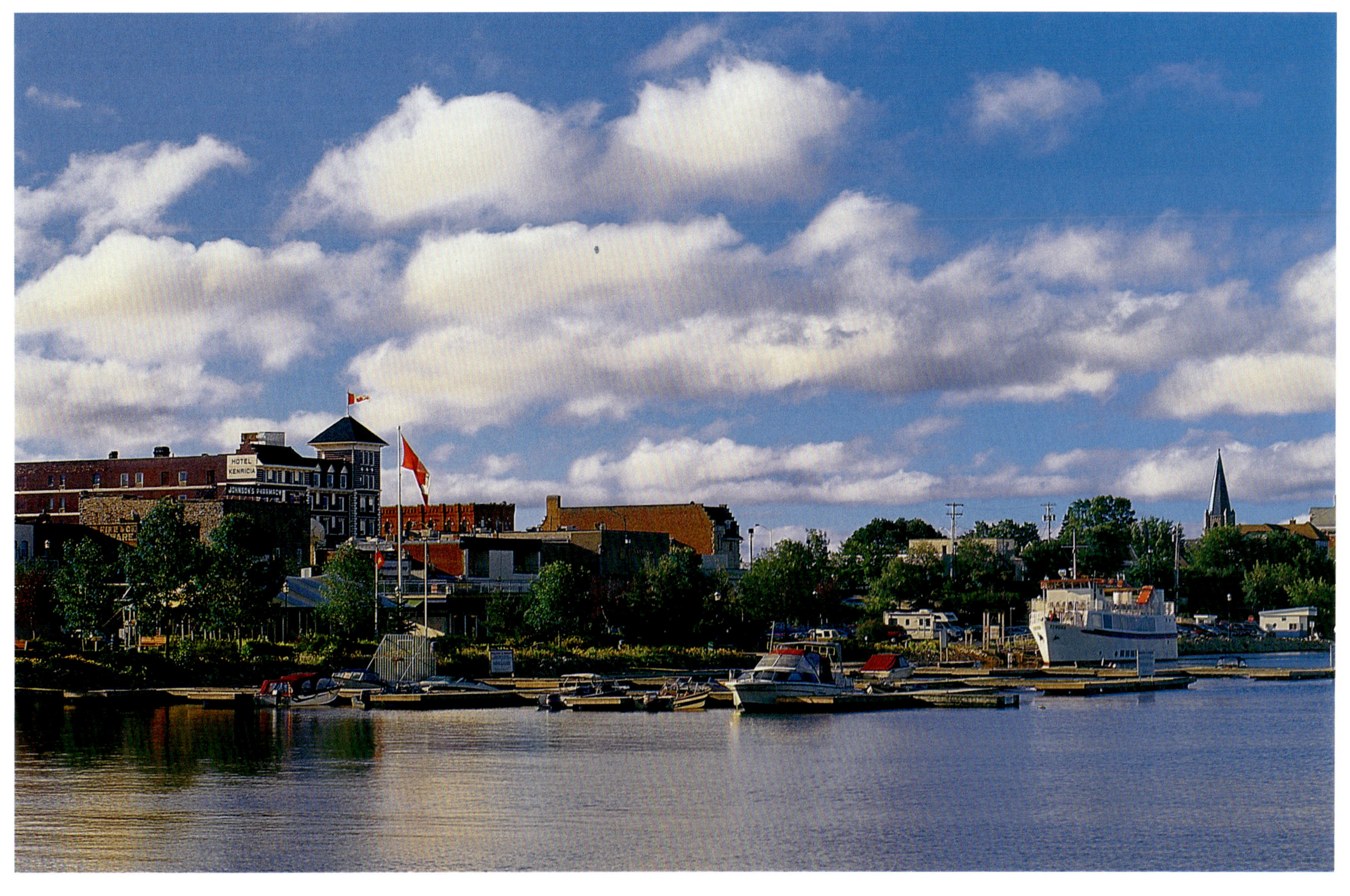

Explorer Jacques De Noyon became the first European to see Lake of the Woods in 1688. Forty years later, La Vérendrye built a French fort in the region.

Golfers at the Kenora Golf and Country Club enjoy panoramic views of Lake of the Woods. The rugged Canadian Shield landscape offers some challenges along the course.

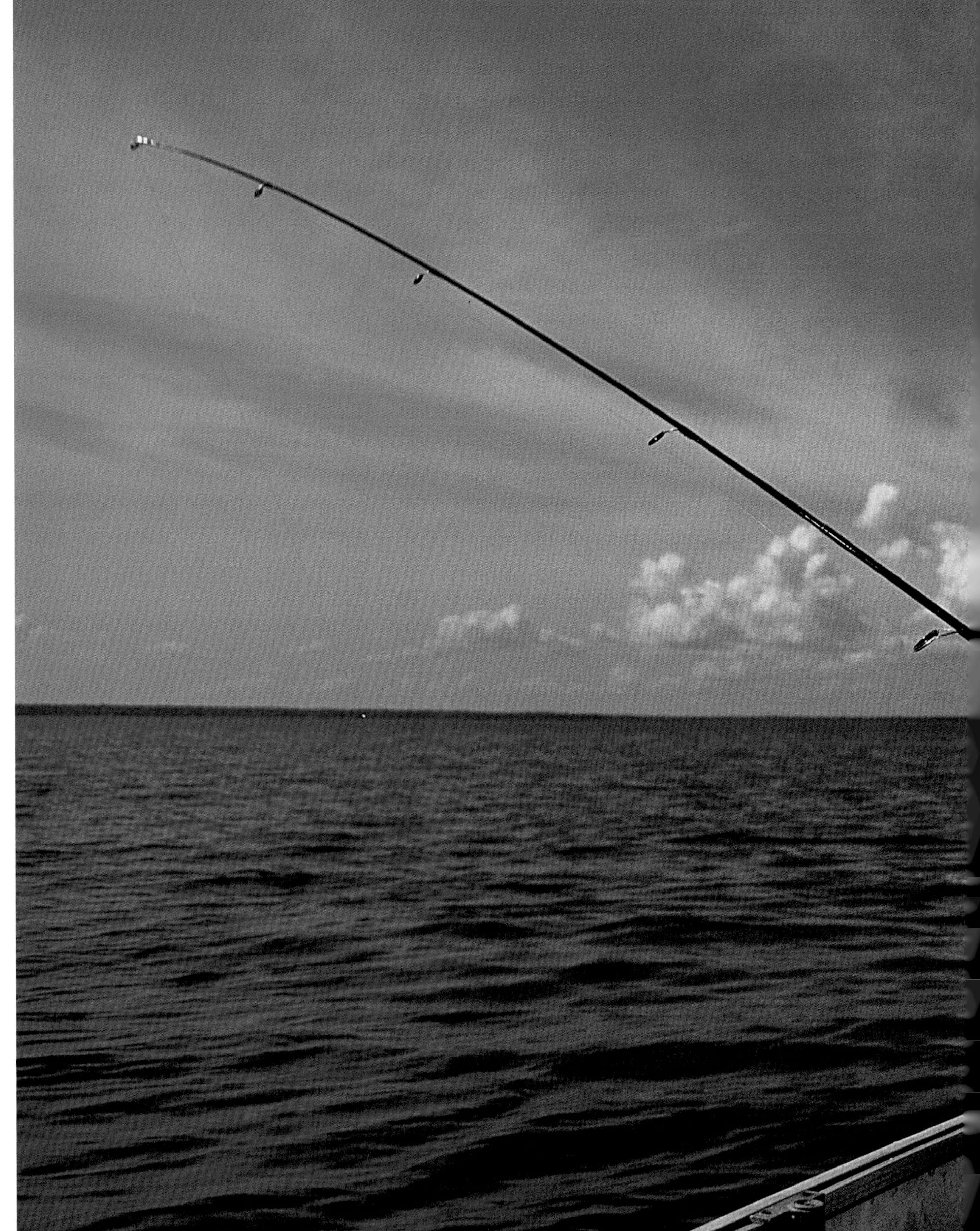

Anglers, hoping for catches of walleye, muskie, and smallmouth bass from the waters of Lake of the Woods, are part of a long history of fishing in the region. In the late 1800s, commercial vessels plied these waters, harvesting the world's largest supply of caviar.

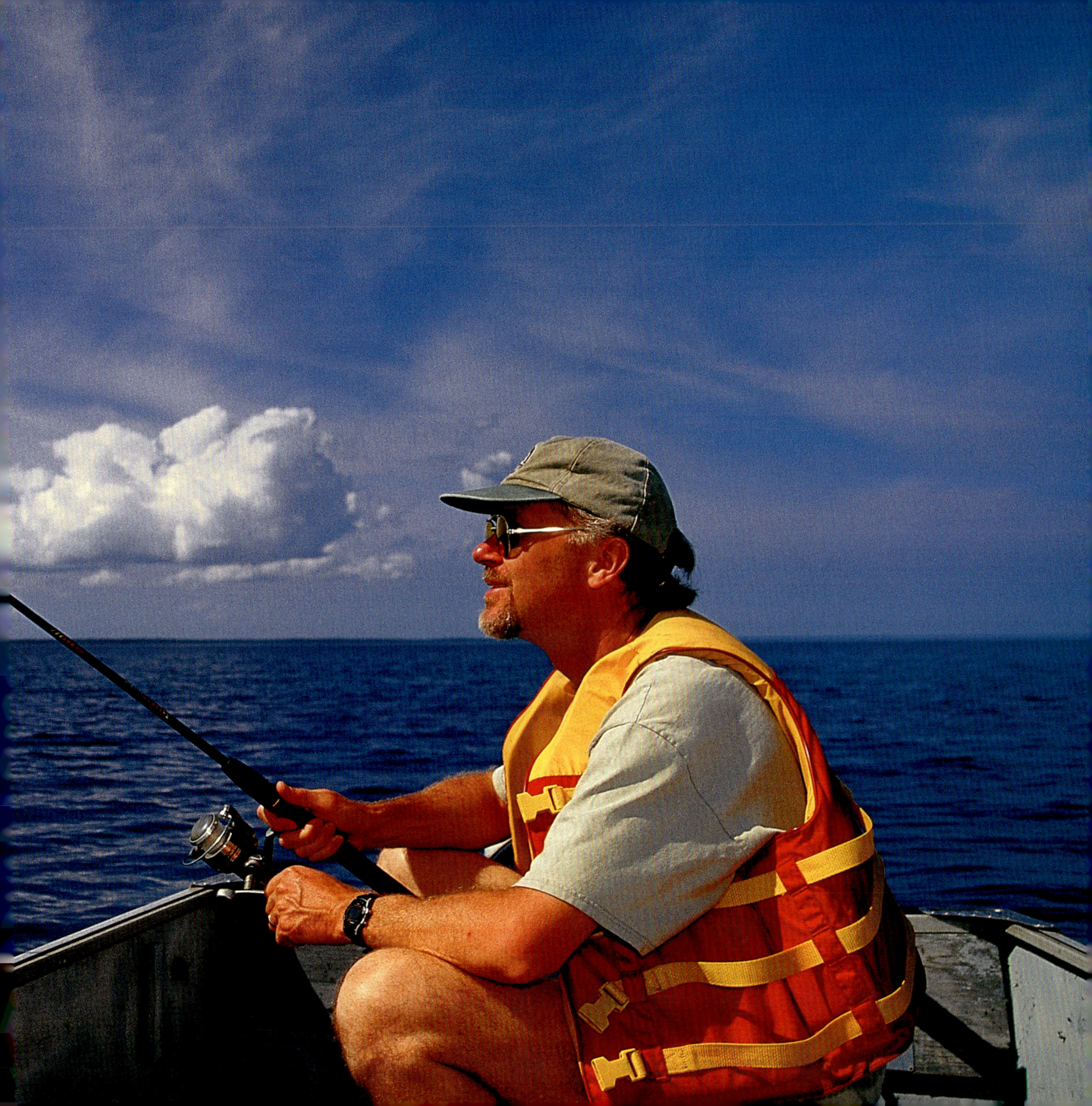

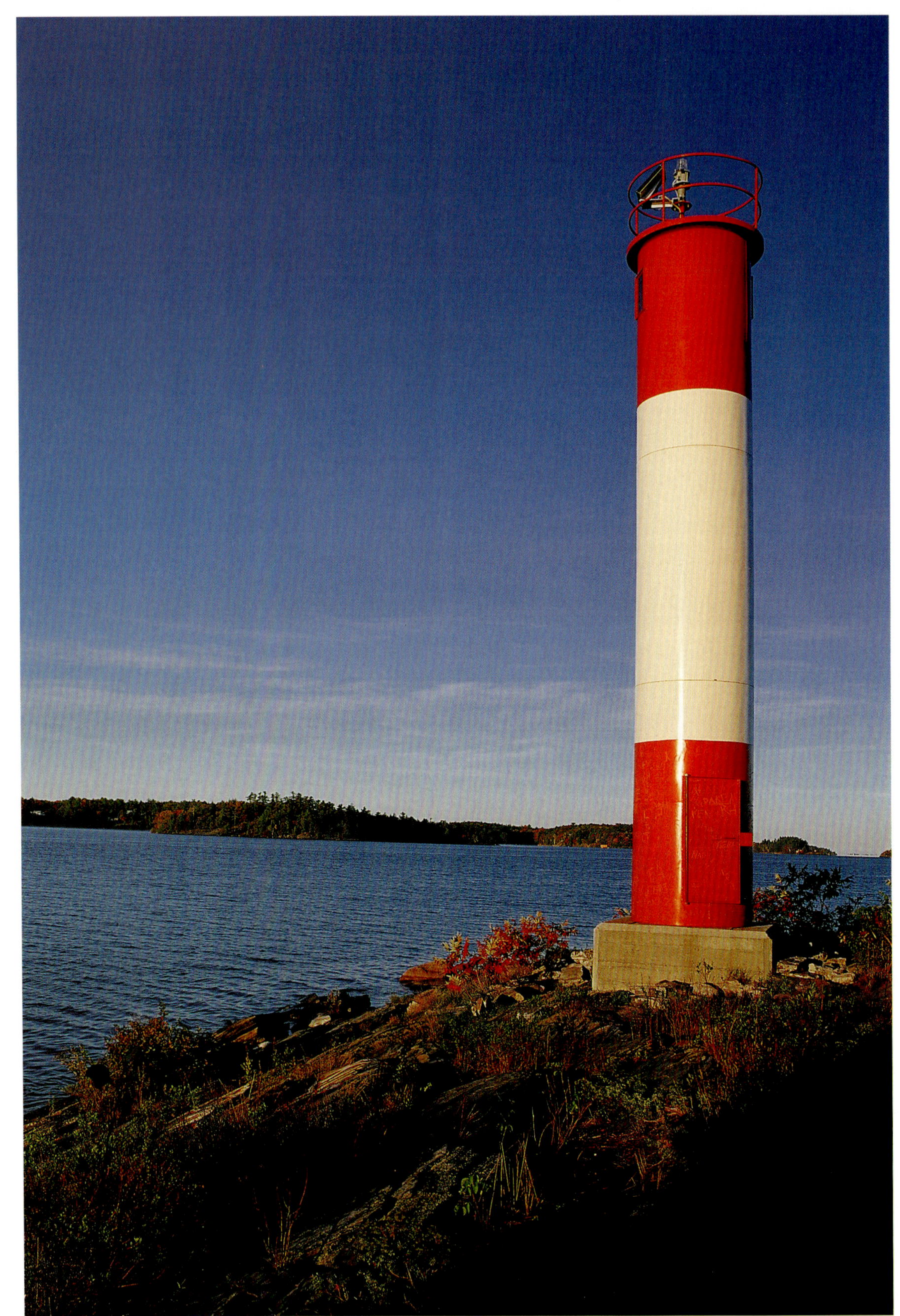

Killbear Provincial Park on Georgian Bay lies on the edge of the Canadian Shield, where rugged shores meet white sand beaches, and the wind-twisted pines so typical of Ontario meet the more delicate shapes of maple and beech. Killbear Lighthouse is almost a century old.

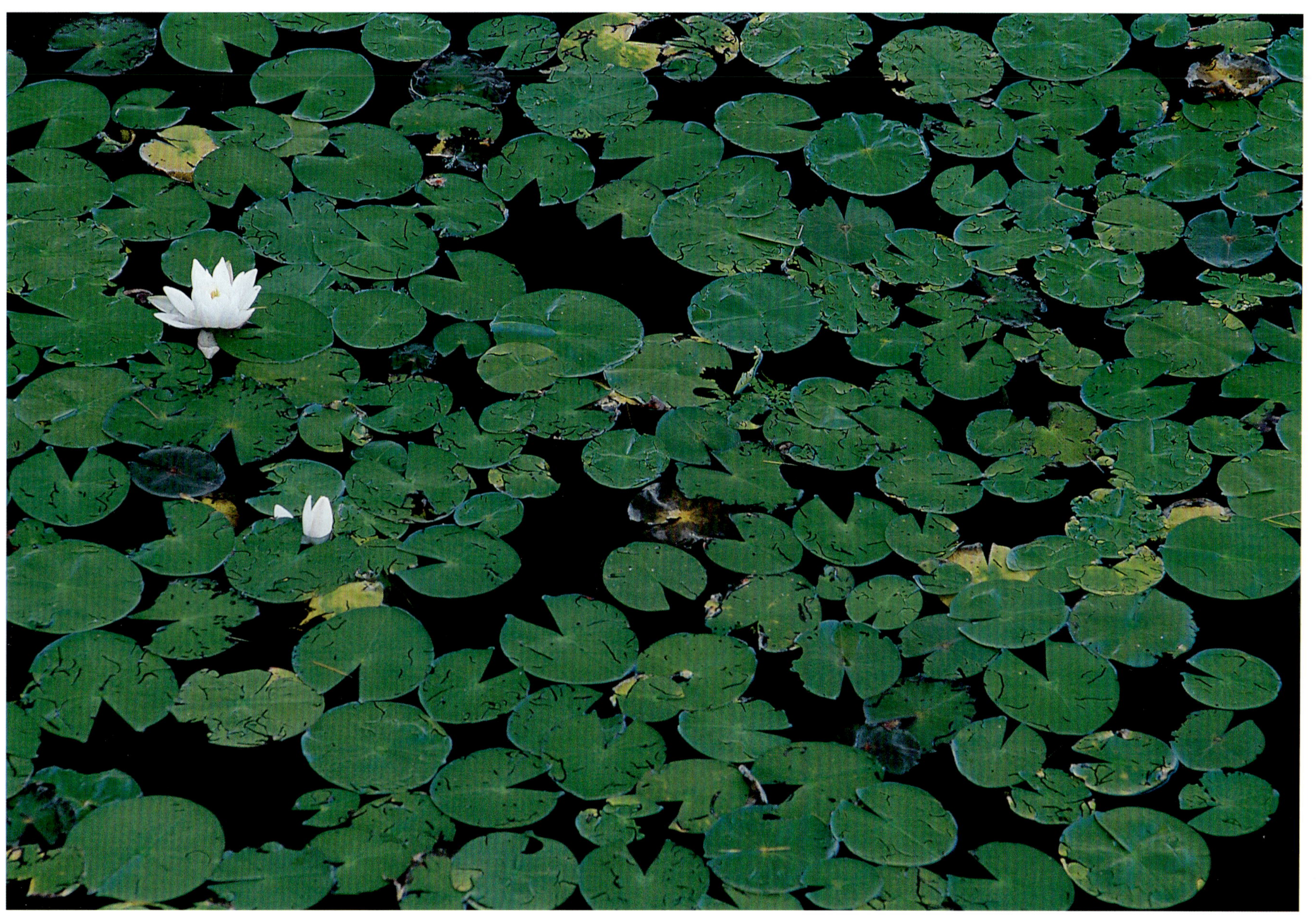

The north shore of Georgian Bay, now protected by Killarney Provincial Park, once inspired the Group of Seven, who spent entire summers camped in the region capturing the rugged landscape on canvas.

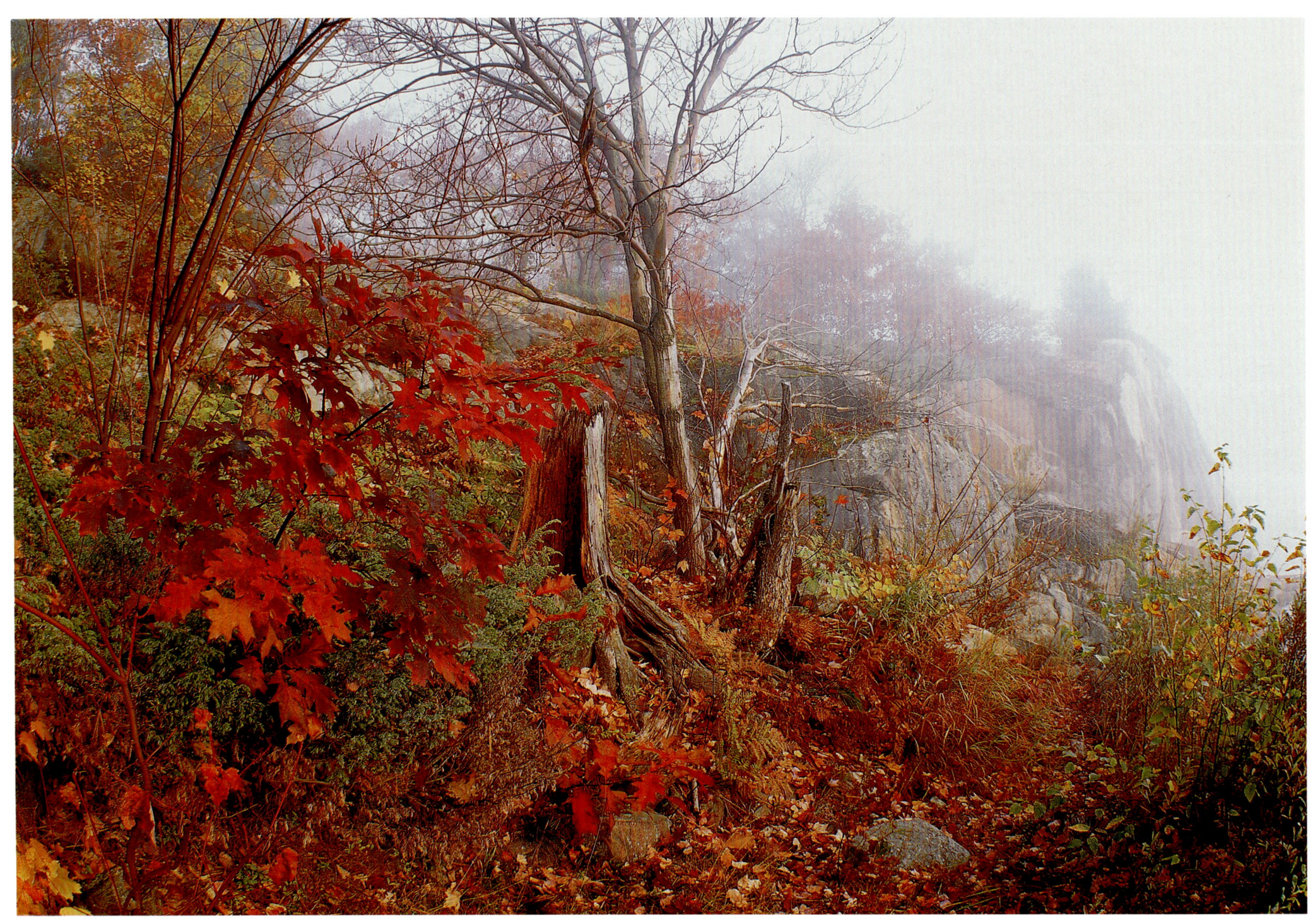

Summer finds experienced hikers skirting Georgian Bay on the La Cloche Silhouette Trail, a challenging 100-kilometre (60-mile) route that takes a week or more to complete. Three shorter trails within Killarney Provincial Park offer alternatives for day hikers.

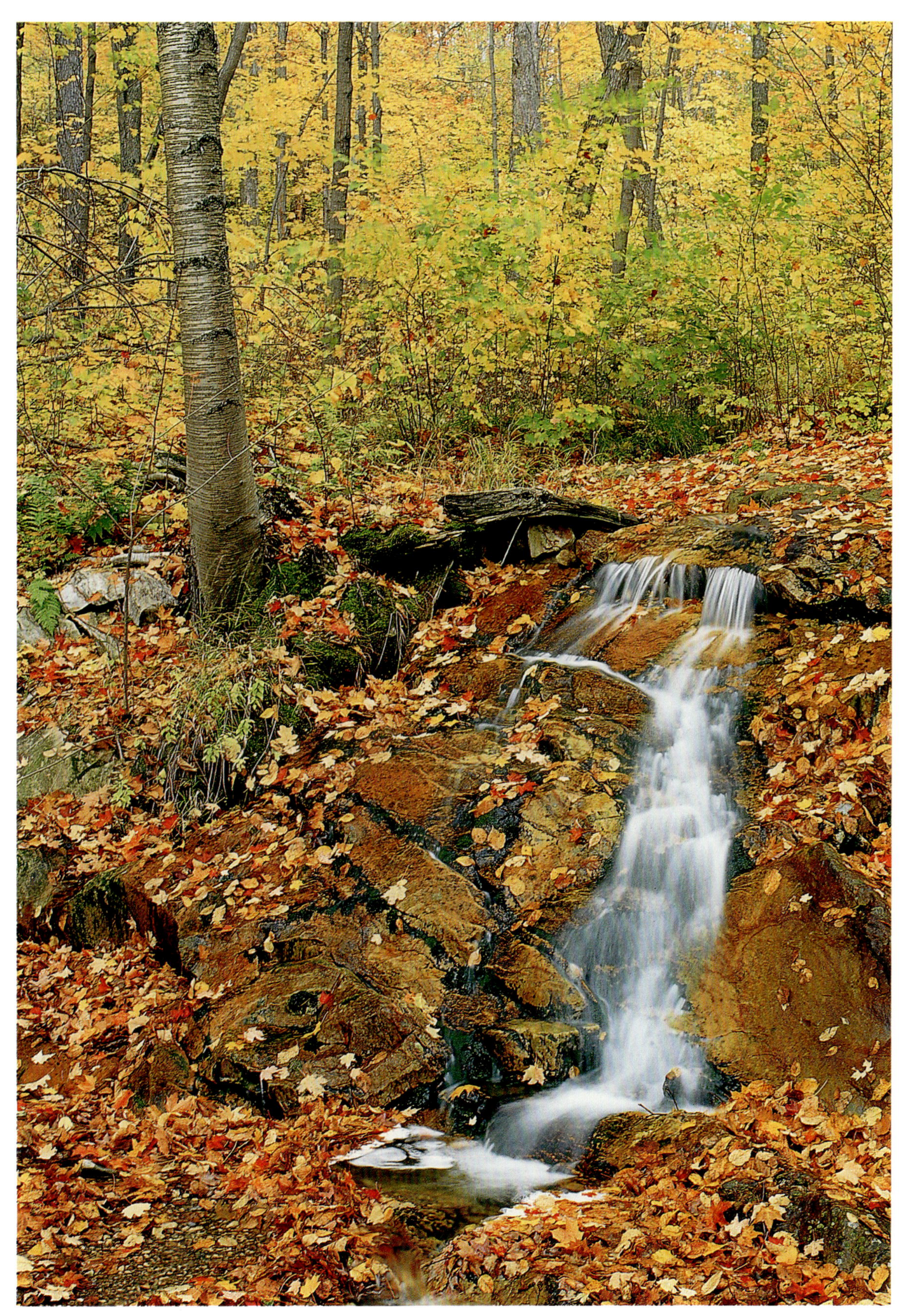

Two billion years ago, the La Cloche Range along Georgian Bay towered higher than the Rocky Mountains. The low but rugged hills of Killarney are part of what remains of those prehistoric peaks.

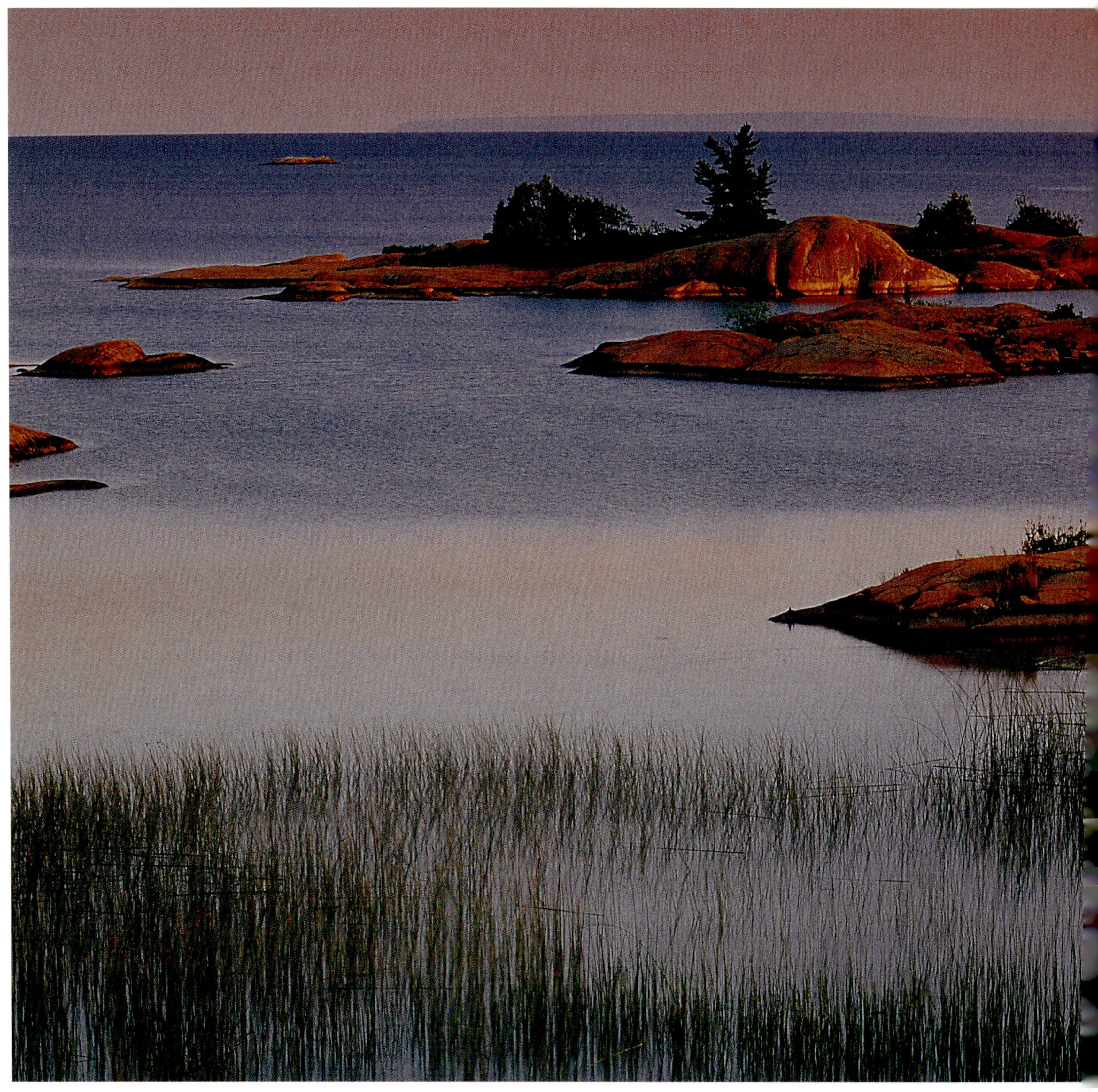

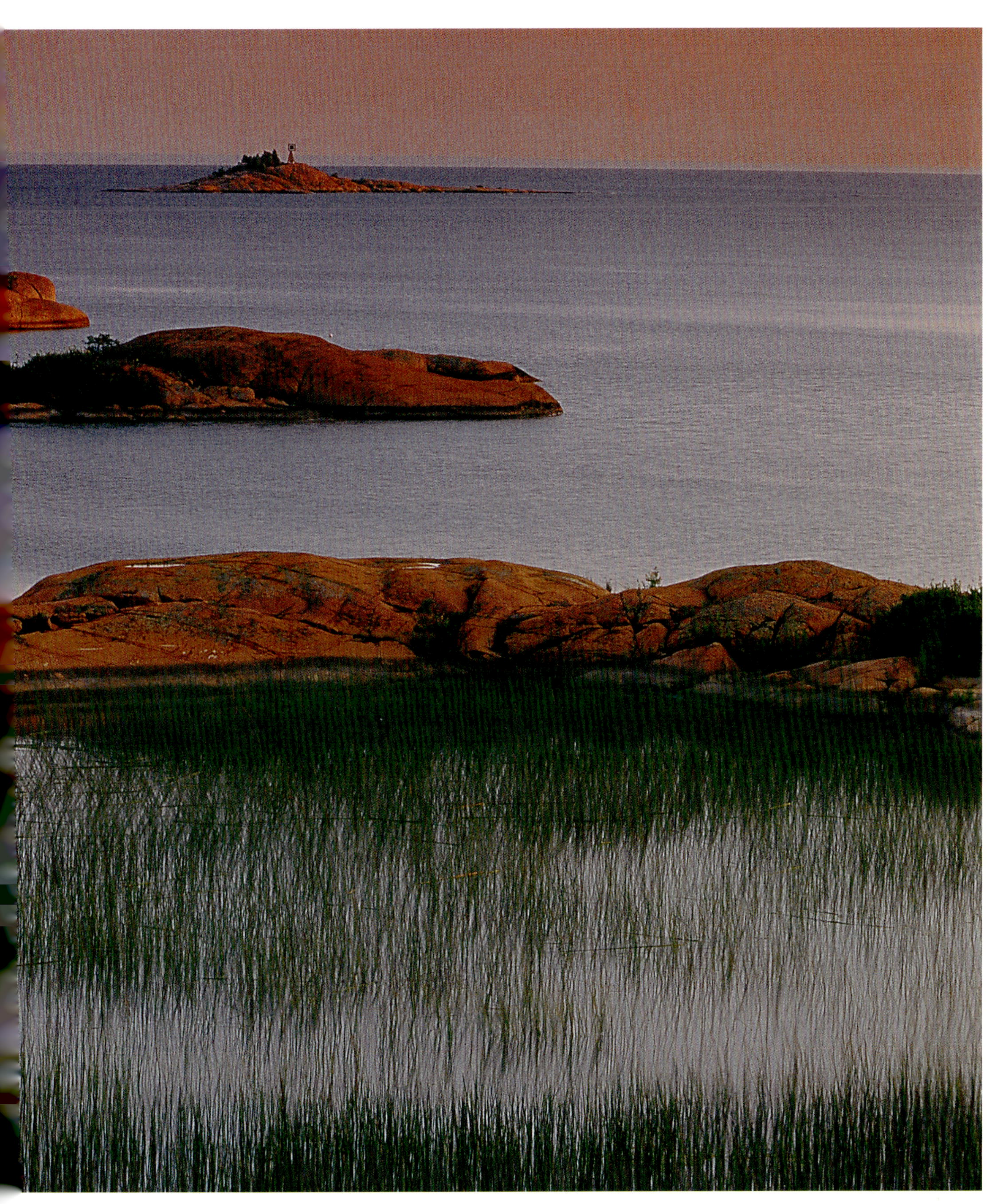

A nearby cottage is a wonderful way to experience Killarney Provincial Park, but it's certainly not essential—almost 300 campsites cater to visitors year round.

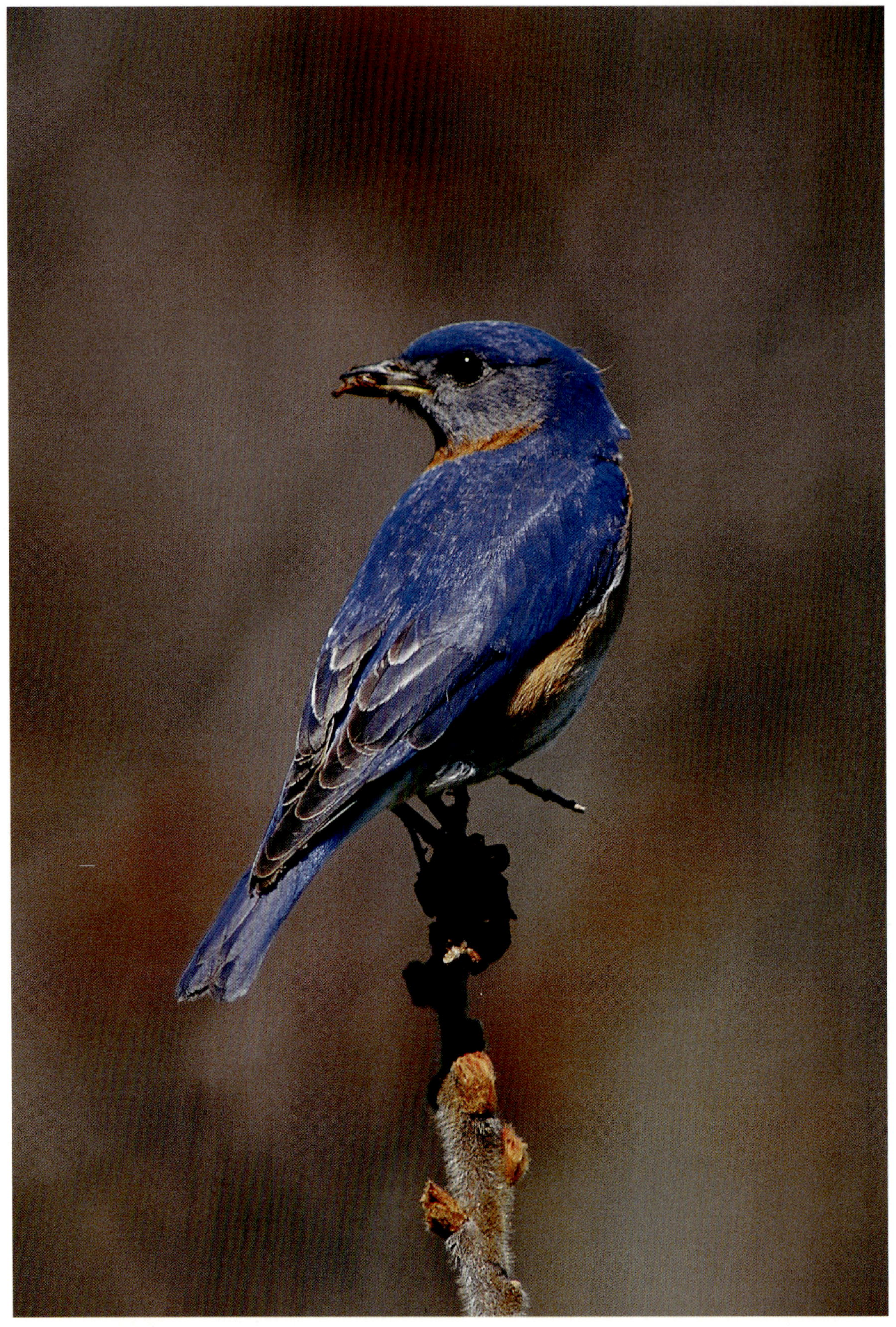

More than 100 bird species breed within Killarney Provincial Park, including the tiny eastern bluebird. About 14 to 18 centimetres (5½ to 7 inches) tall, the songbird is a particularly colourful member of the thrush family.

FACING PAGE—
Once fishing and camping sites for the Huron people, the 30,000 islands along the north and east coasts of Georgian Bay are now home to private cottages and camps. Twenty-nine of the islands are protected as part of Georgian Bay Islands National Park.

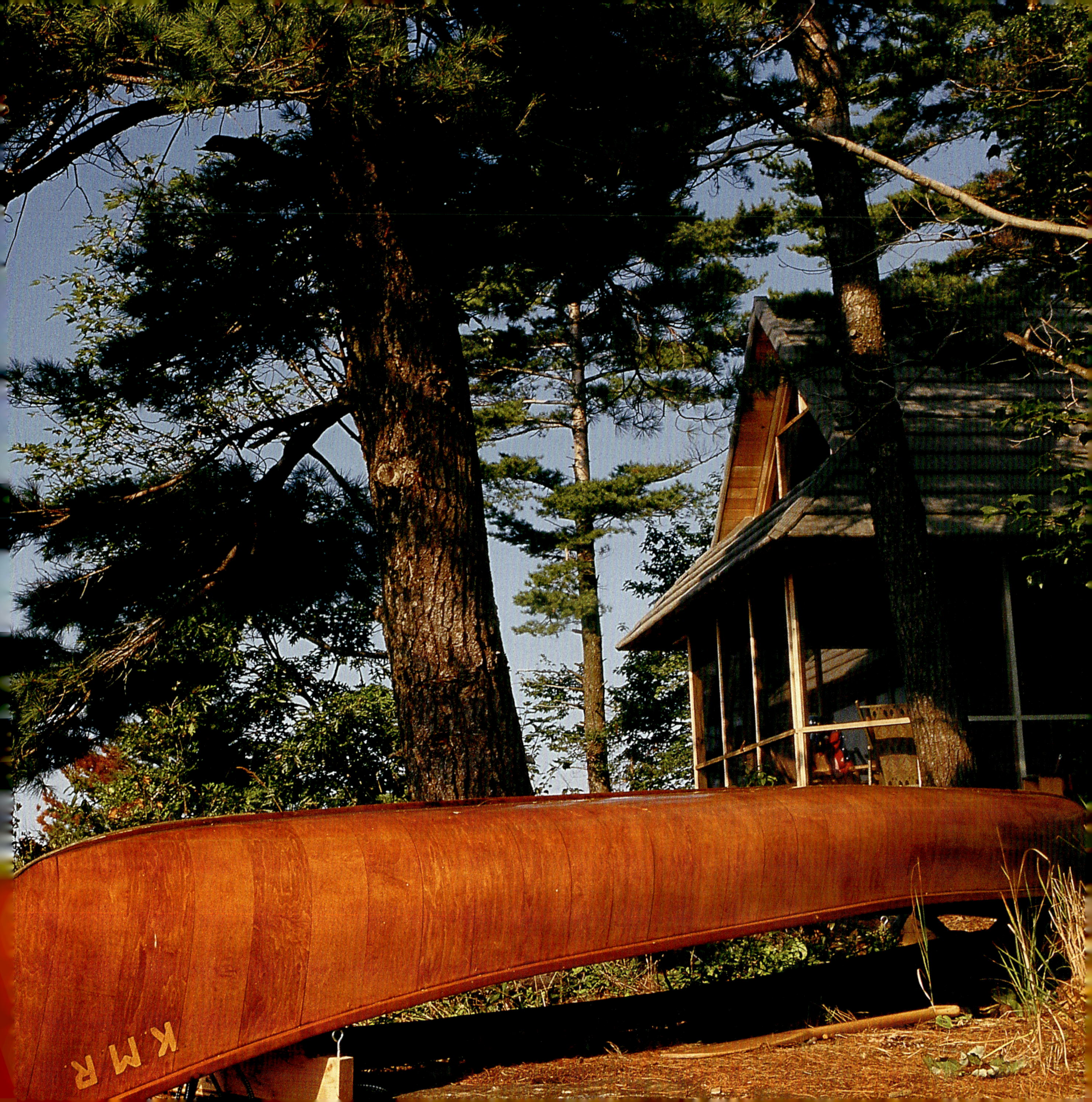
KMR

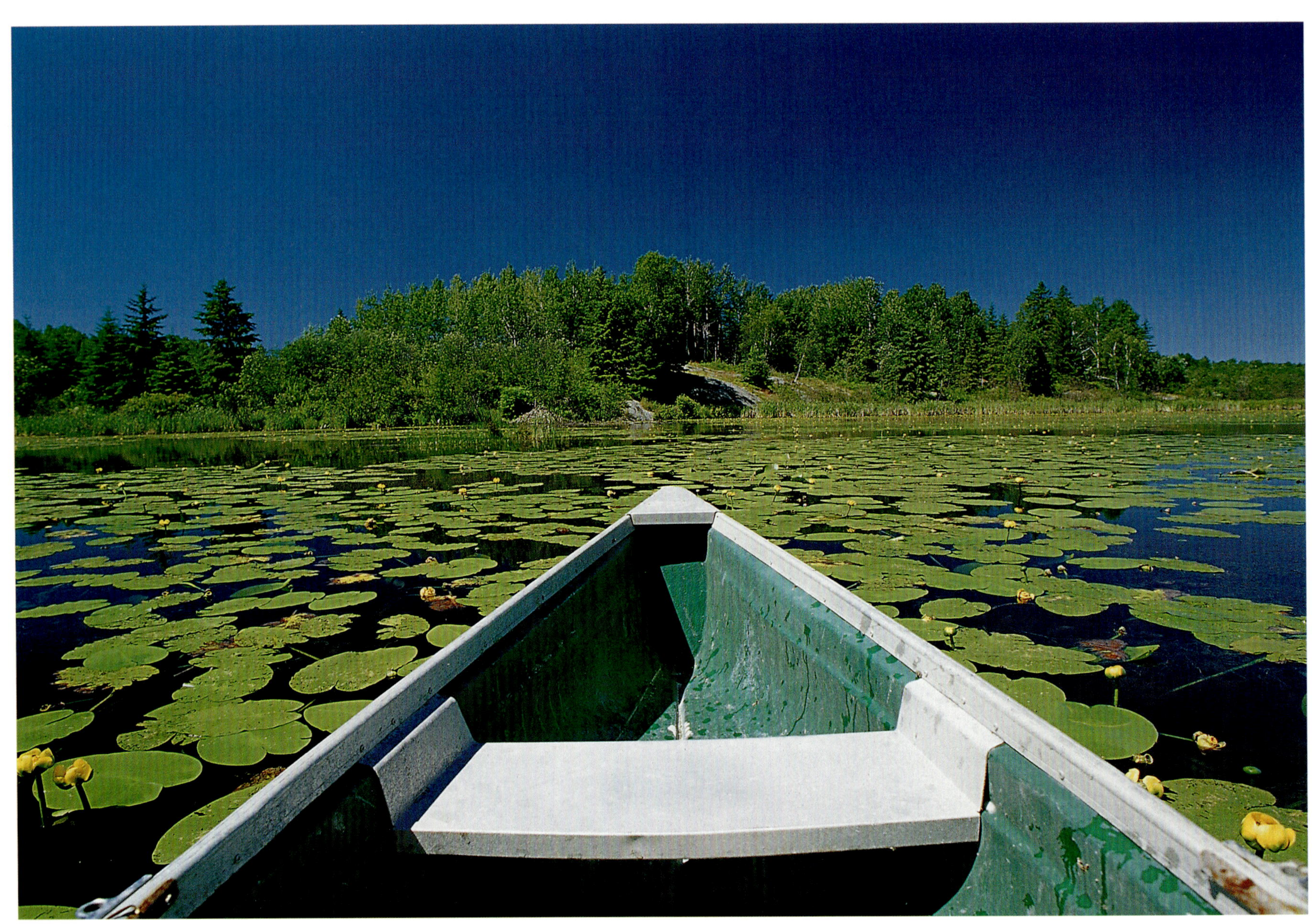

The landscape of the Canadian Shield, rocky outcroppings interrupted by glacial lakes and swift rivers, extends from the shores of Hudson Bay to the northern reaches of the United States and east as far as Labrador. It encompasses nearly half the nation—4.6 million square kilometres (1.8 million square miles).

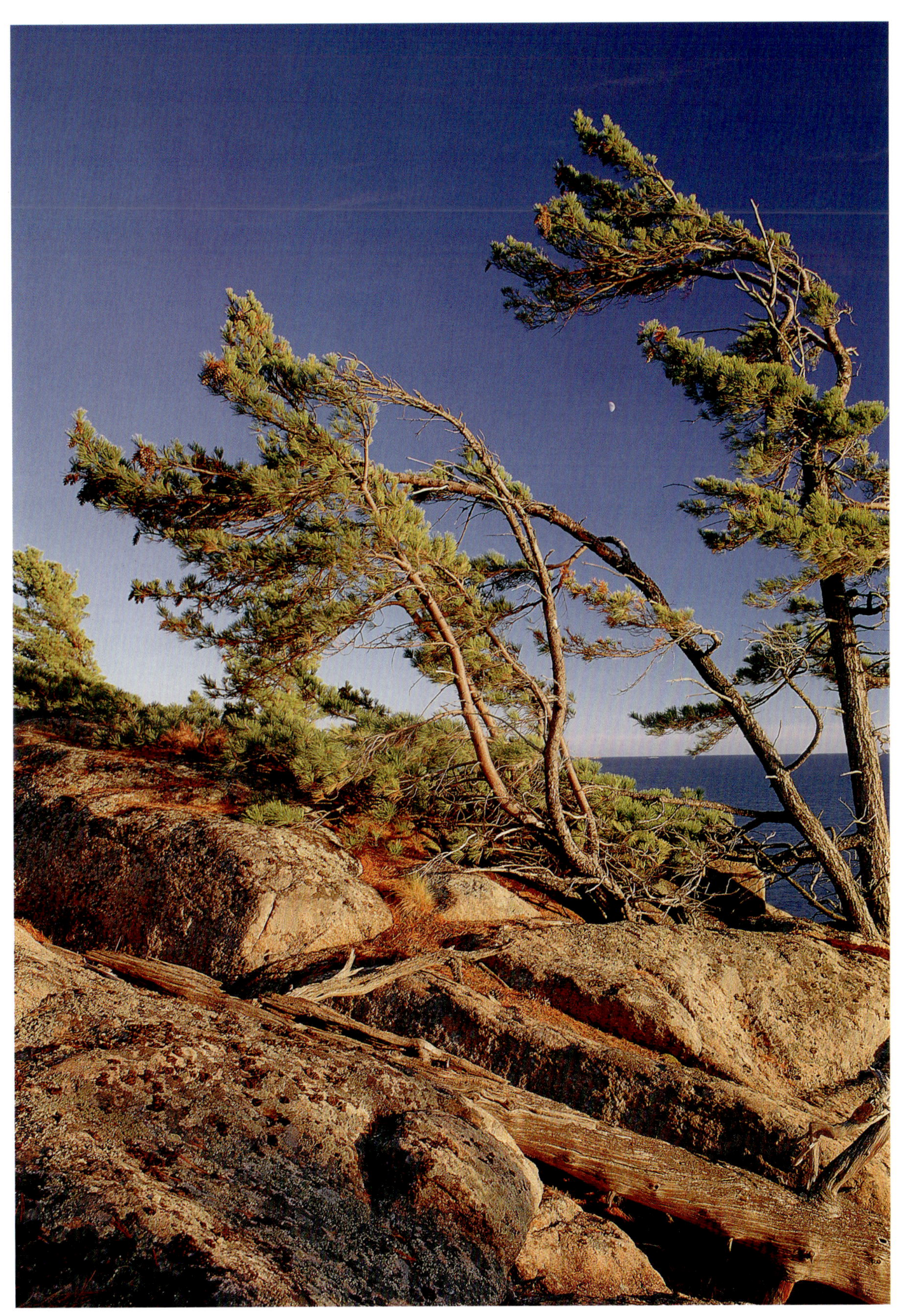

Hardy white pines manage to survive the harsh climate on the shores of Georgian Bay, along with junipers and red oak. On the rocks below, vibrant lichens slowly scratch away at the stone.

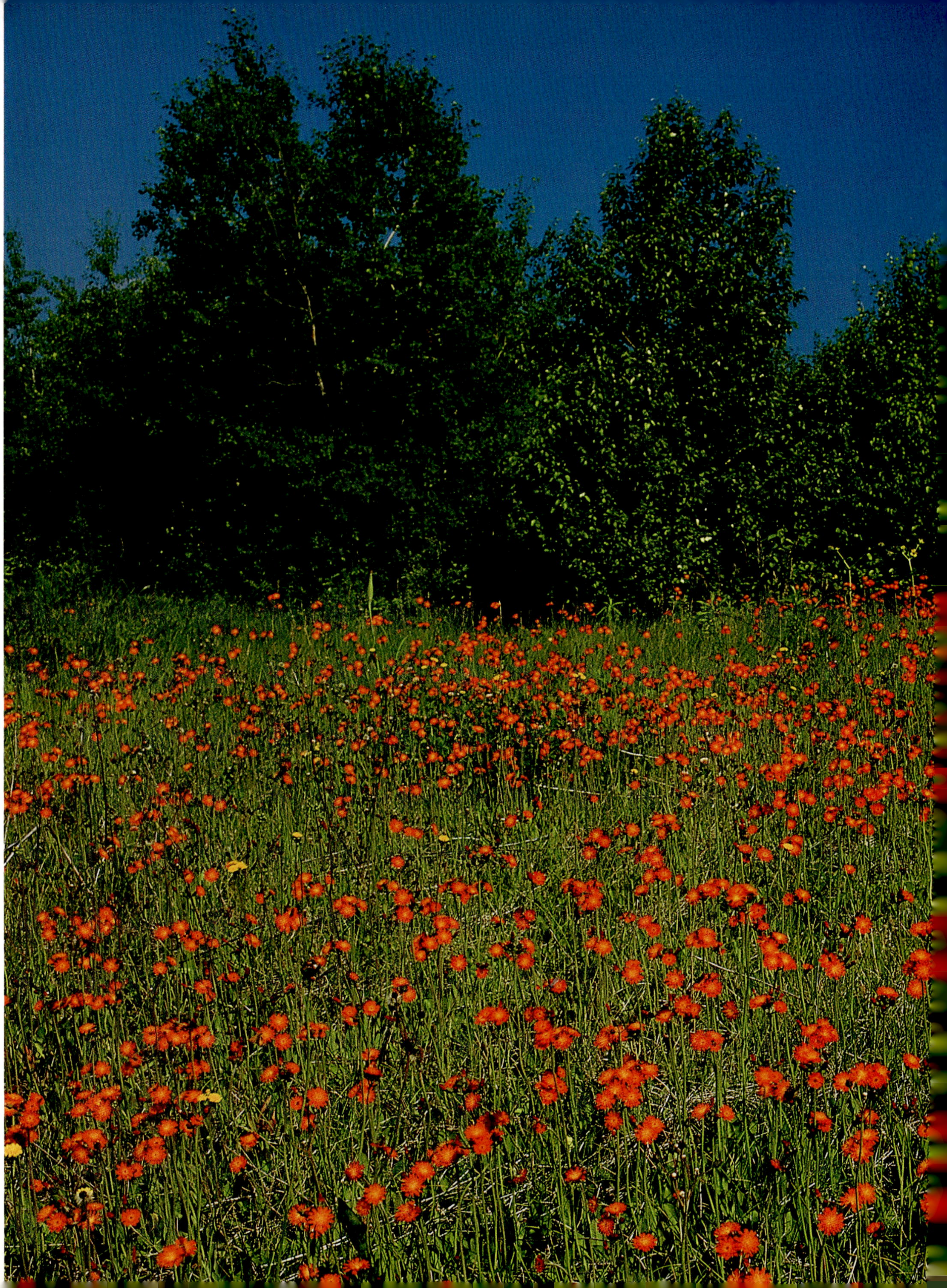

Orange hawkweed carpets a field near Whitefish. This tenacious plant with its vibrant flowers was introduced to North America by early European settlers. It now thrives throughout the eastern United States and Canada.

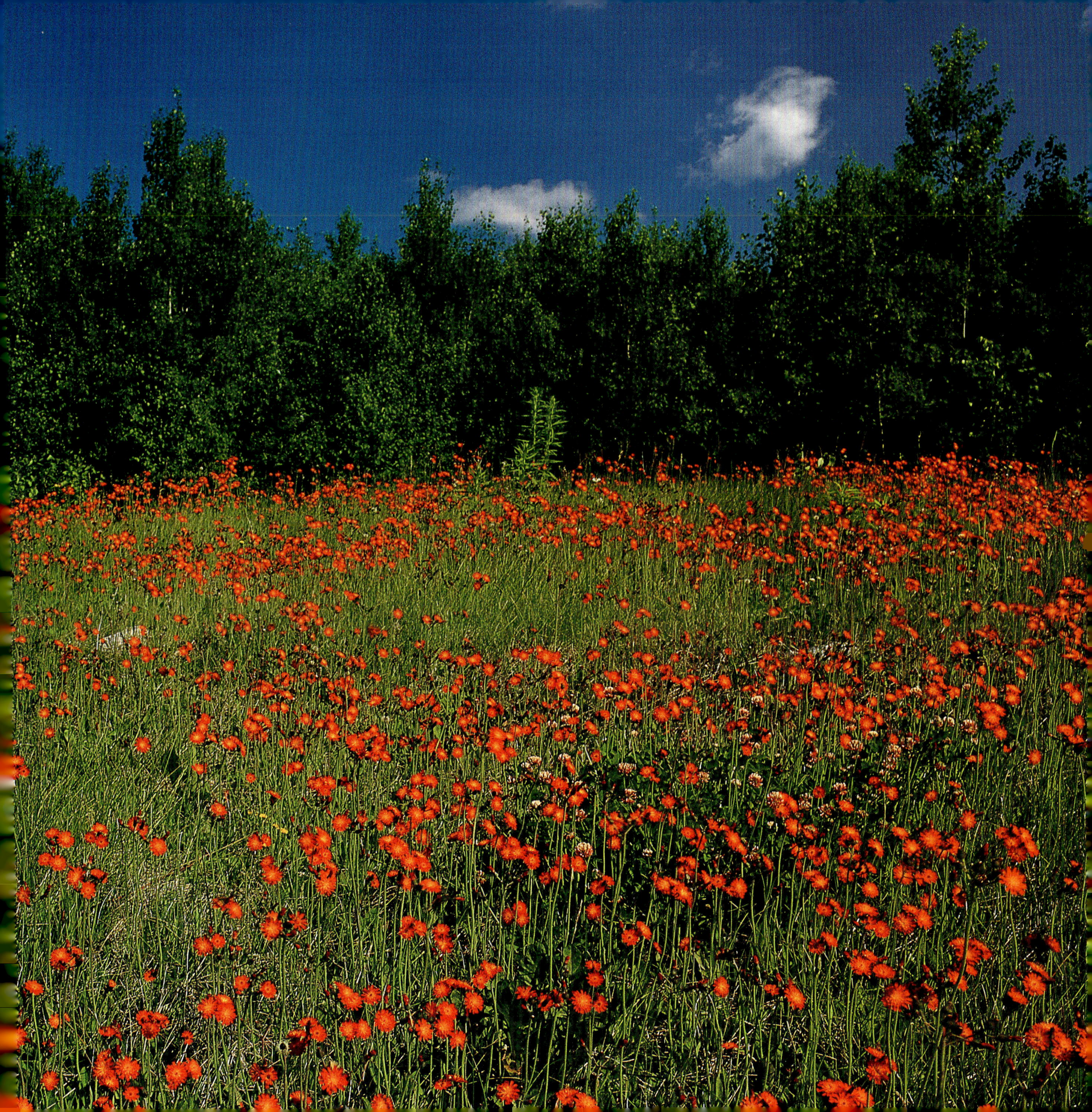

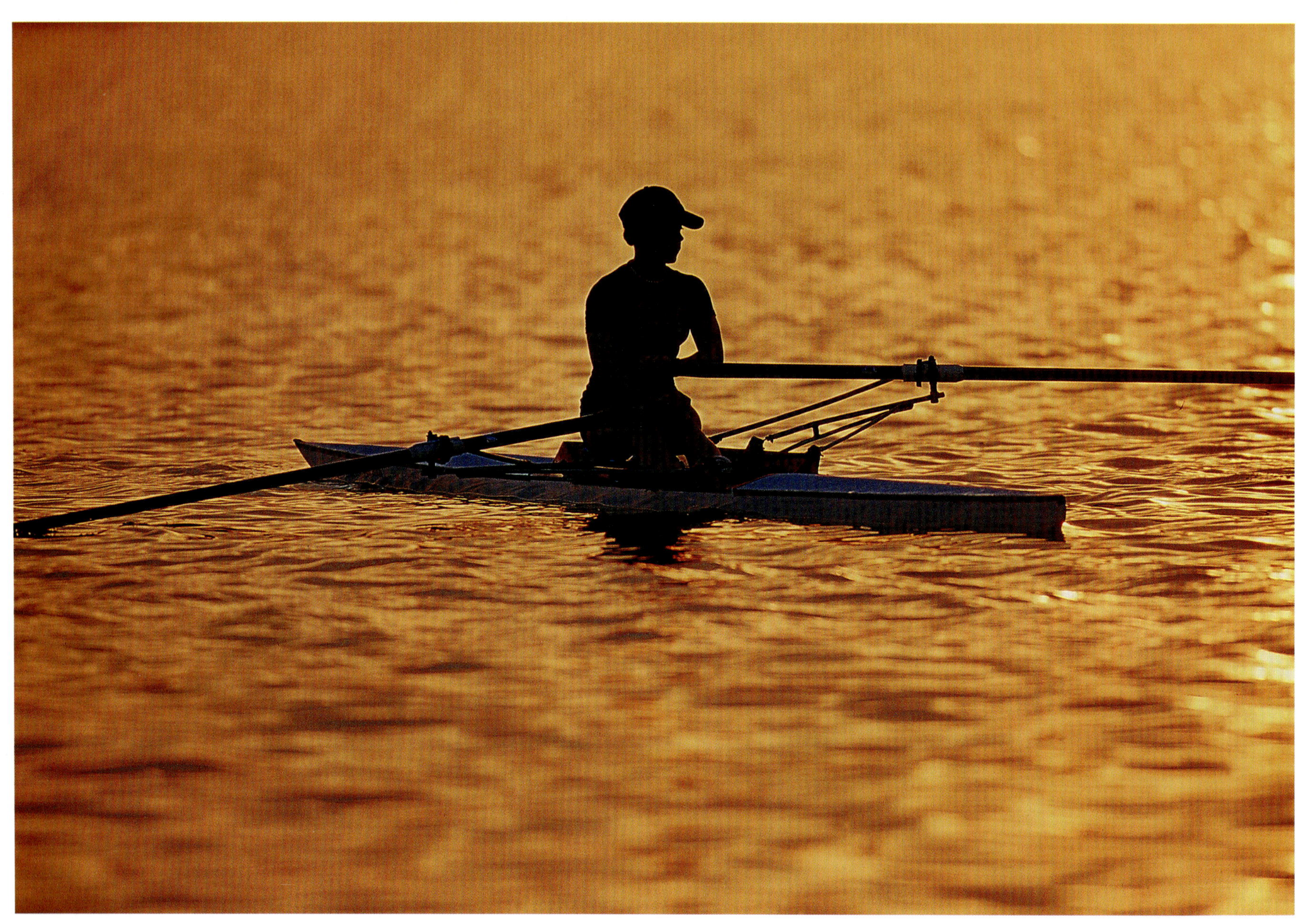

A summer escape to the lake isn't always a long excursion. Lake Ramsey in Sudbury is the largest lake on the continent that is completely contained within a city. Many of Ontario's schoolchildren have enjoyed the lake's southern shores as guests of Camp Sudaca.

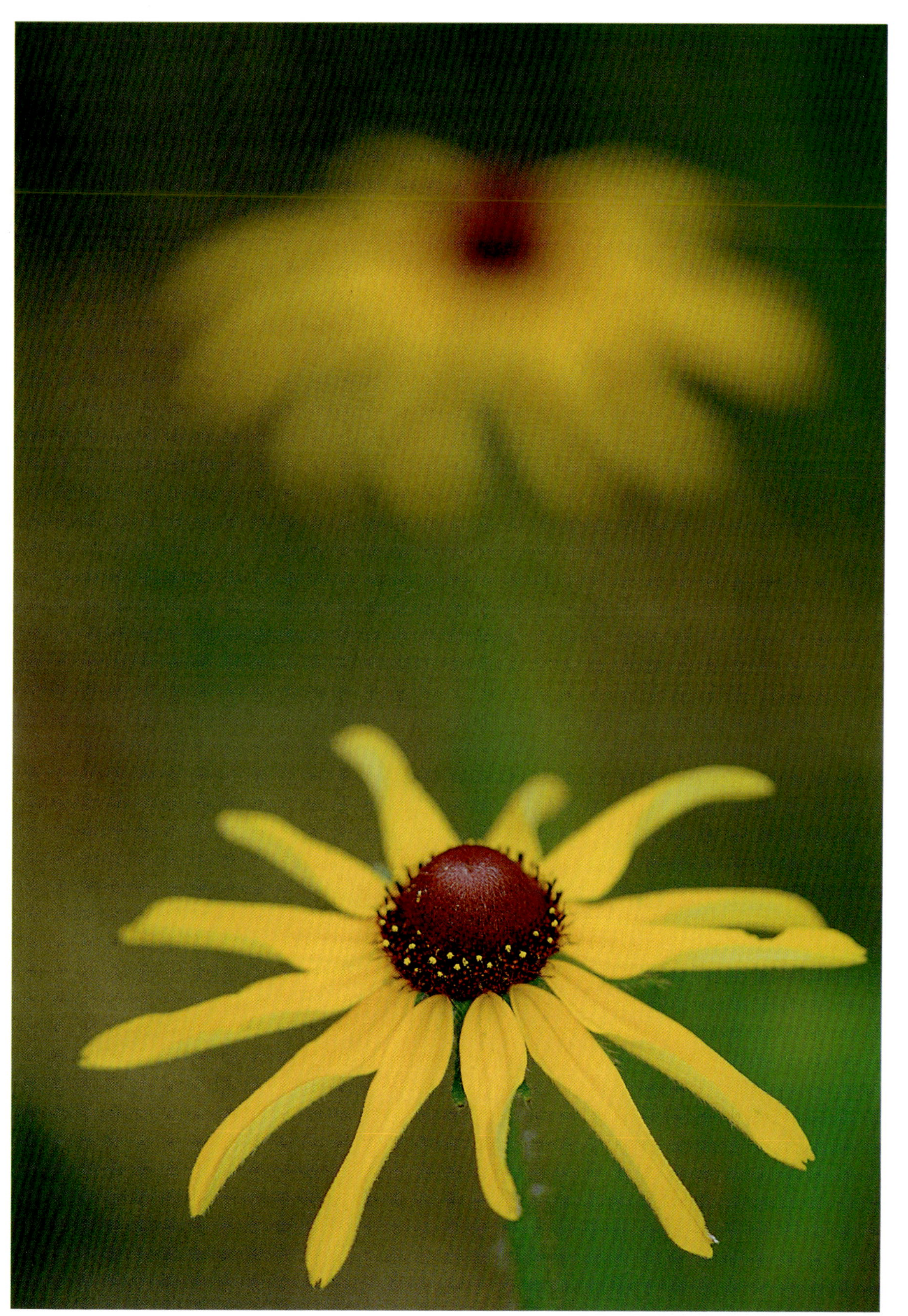

Perennials native to southern Ontario, black-eyed susans bloom throughout the summer months. Popular in gardens, the hardy flowers also thrive in open spaces throughout the forests, able to withstand poor soil or harsh winds, with little or plentiful water.

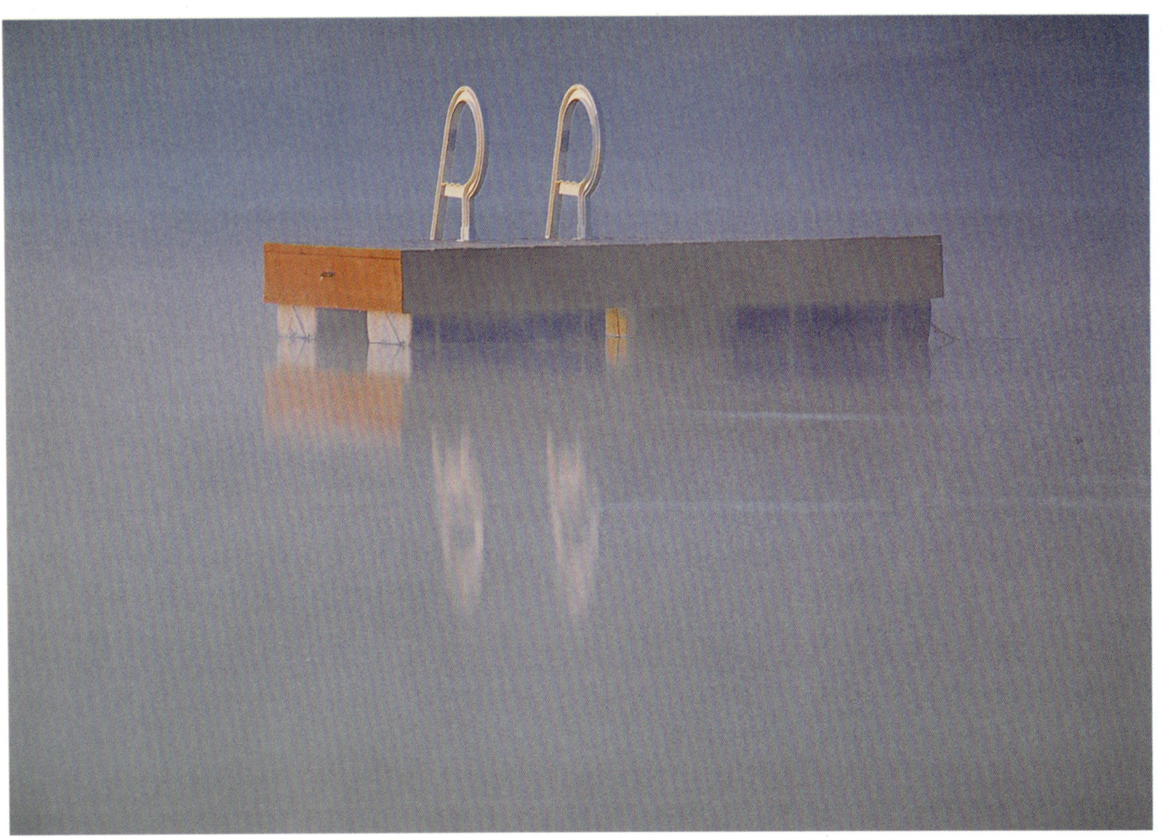

More than 30 million international visitors flock each year to Ontario, some to experience the metropolitan thrills of Toronto or the sights of the Niagara Peninsula, and some to retreat to the campsites, canoe routes, and hiking trails of the province's pristine parks.

From late summer until spring, cottagers occasionally glimpse the northern lights. Caused by particles in solar wind hitting the earth's atmosphere, the lights dance 95 to 130 kilometres (60 to 80 miles) above the earth.

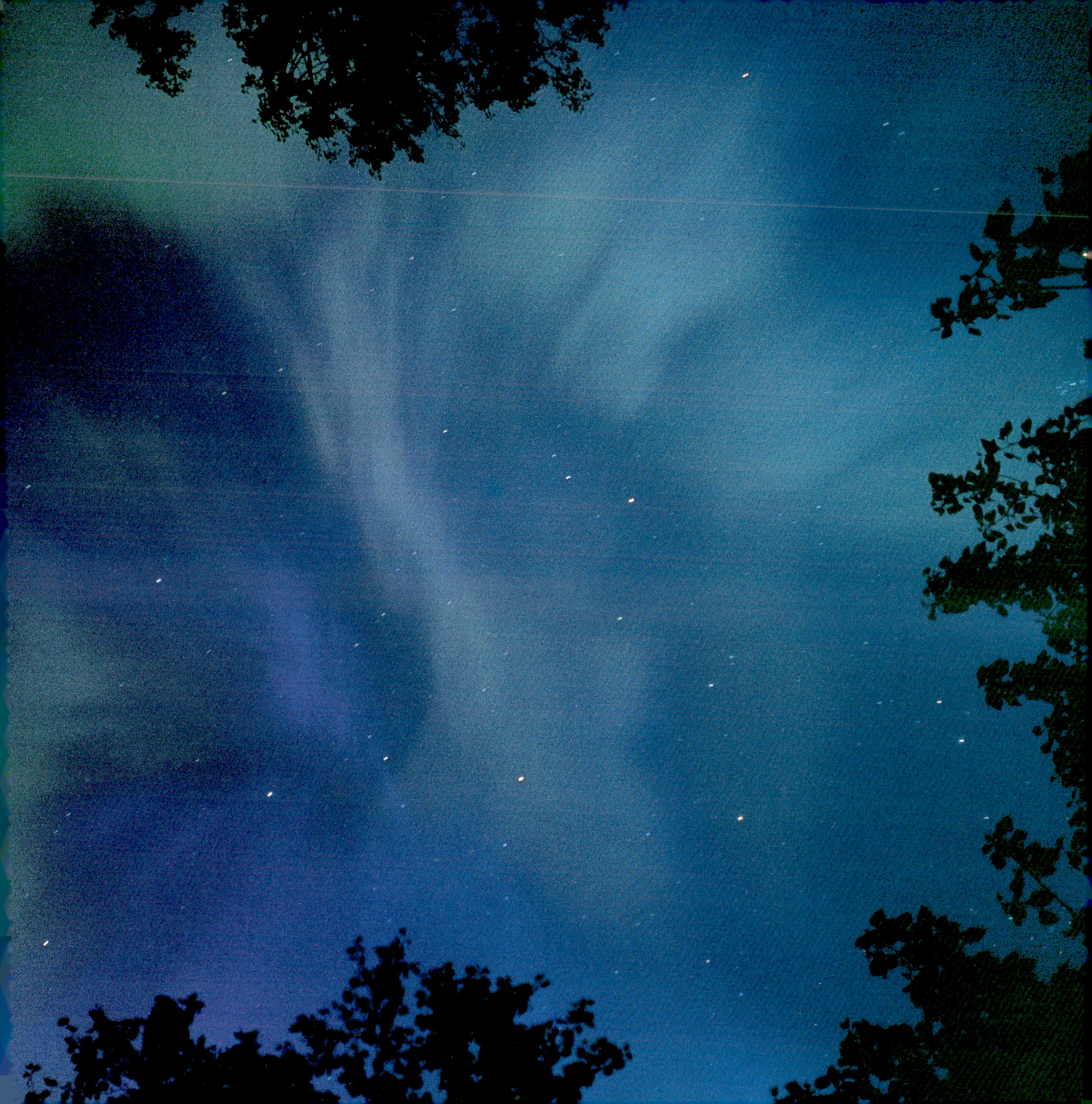

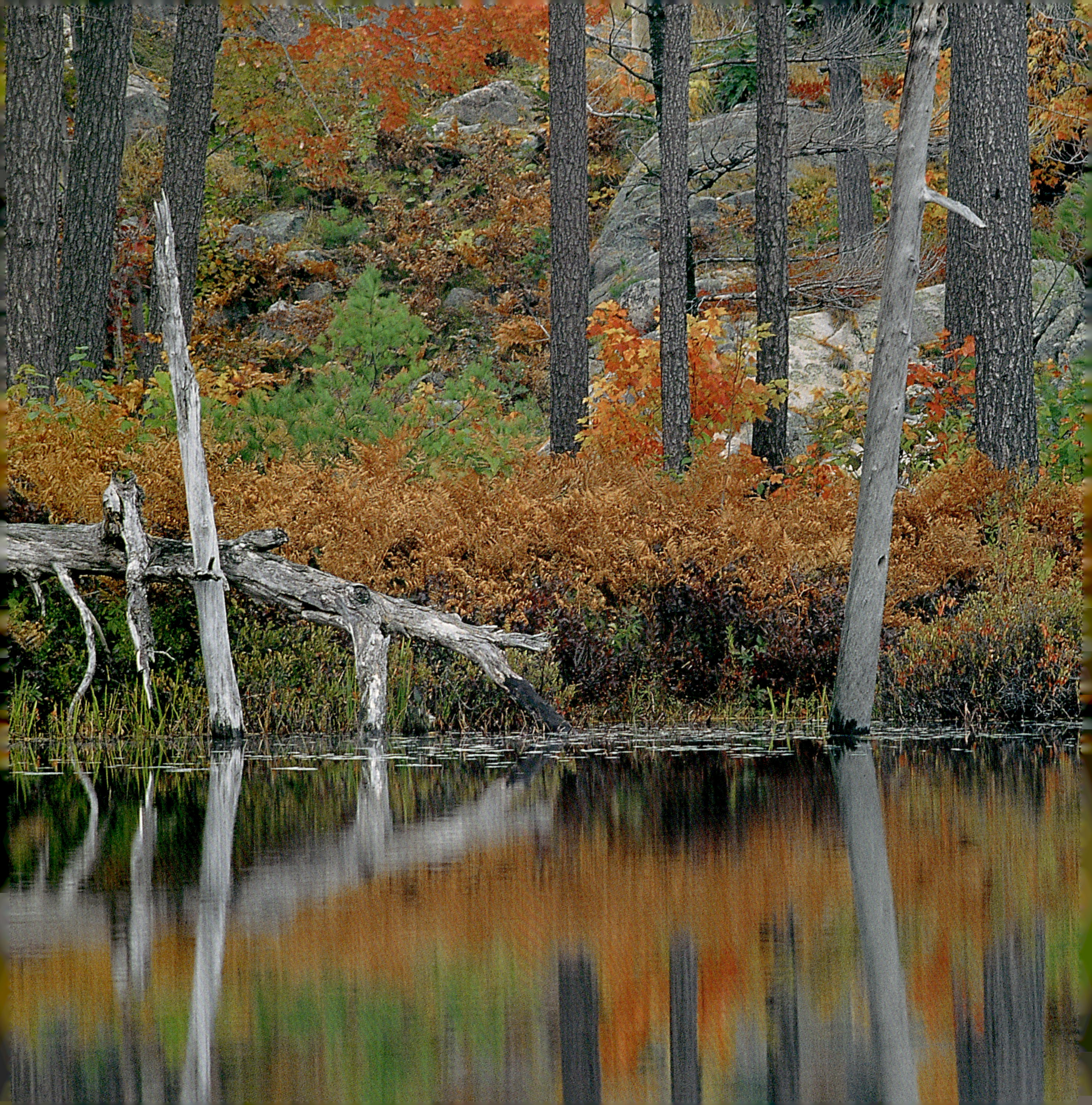

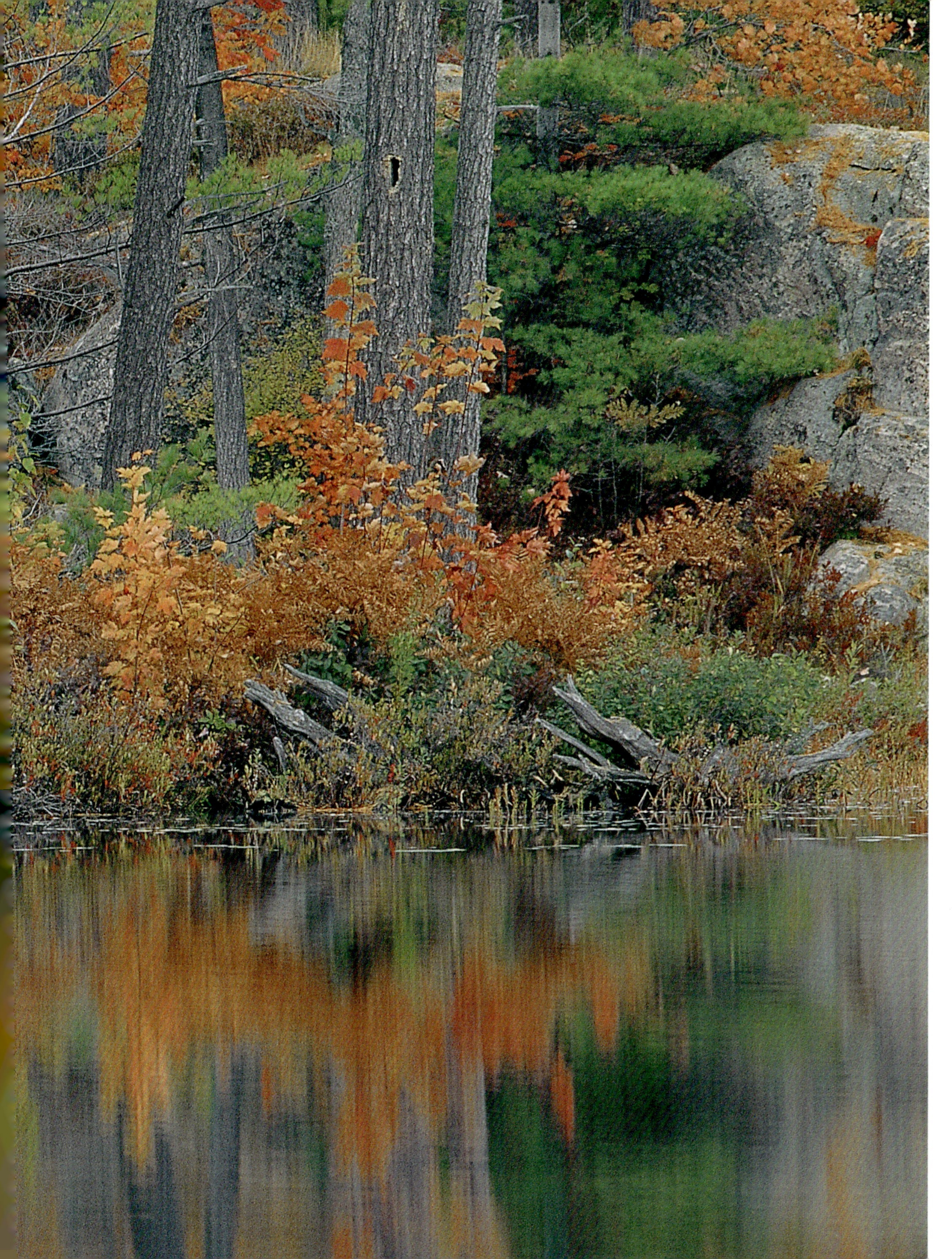

Lake Huron and Georgian Bay boast 6,160 kilometres (3,830 miles) of shoreline. Together, the Great Lakes contain 22,680 cubic kilometres (5,440 cubic miles) of water, one-fifth of the fresh water in the world.

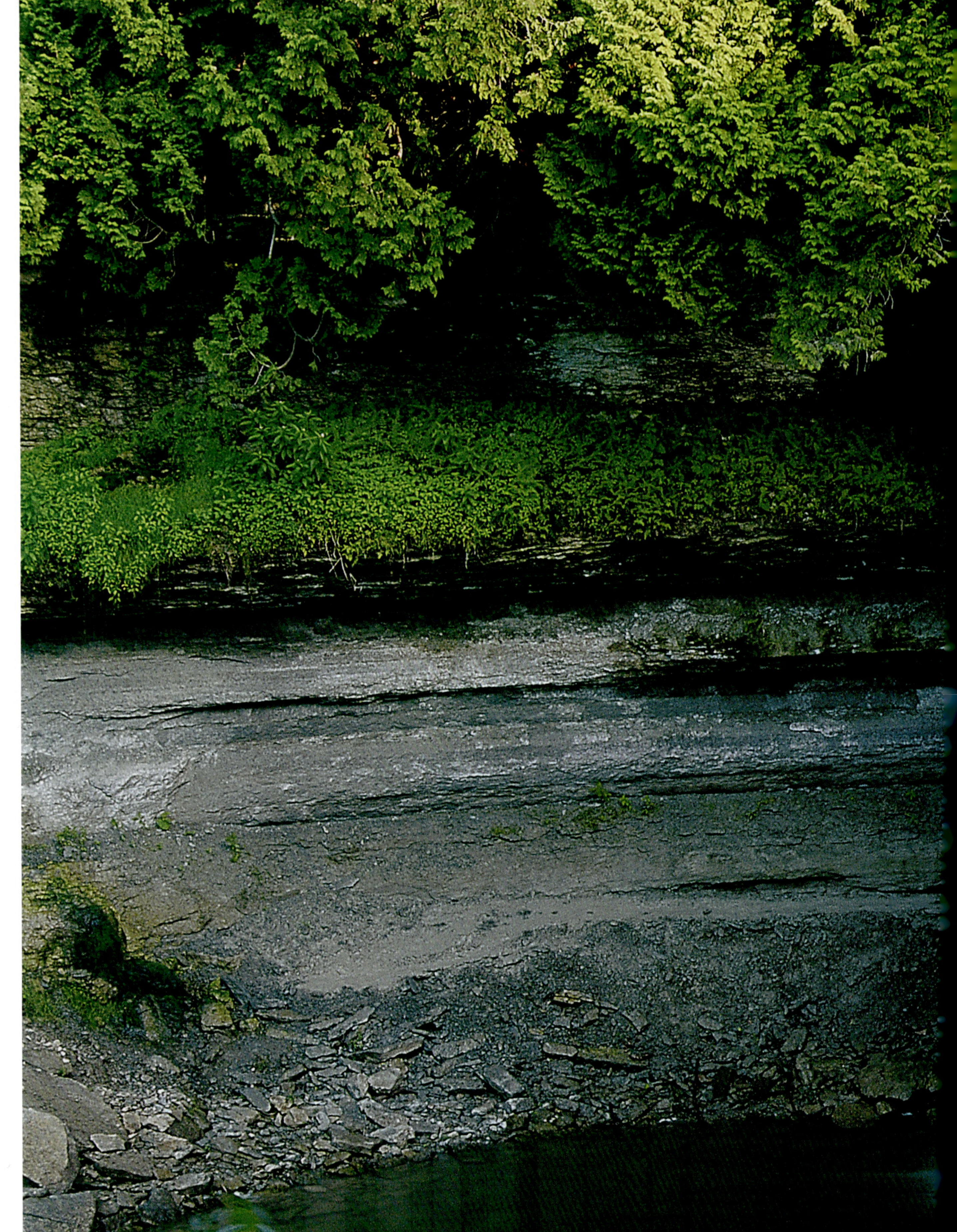

A short hike on Manitoulin Island brings visitors to Bridal Veil Falls, where huge millstones serve as a reminder of the grist mill that once stood here and the early settlers who farmed the island's fertile soils.

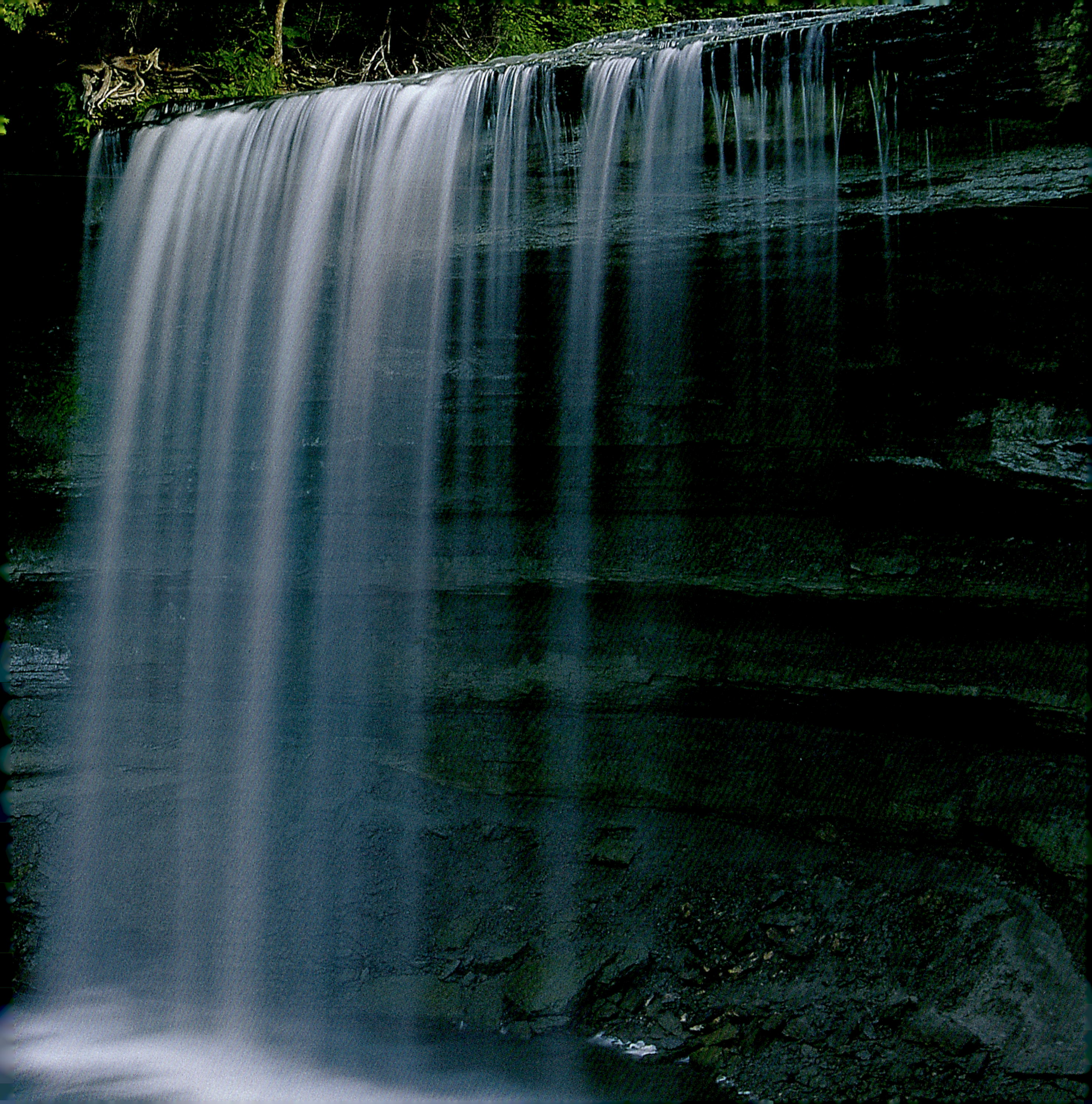

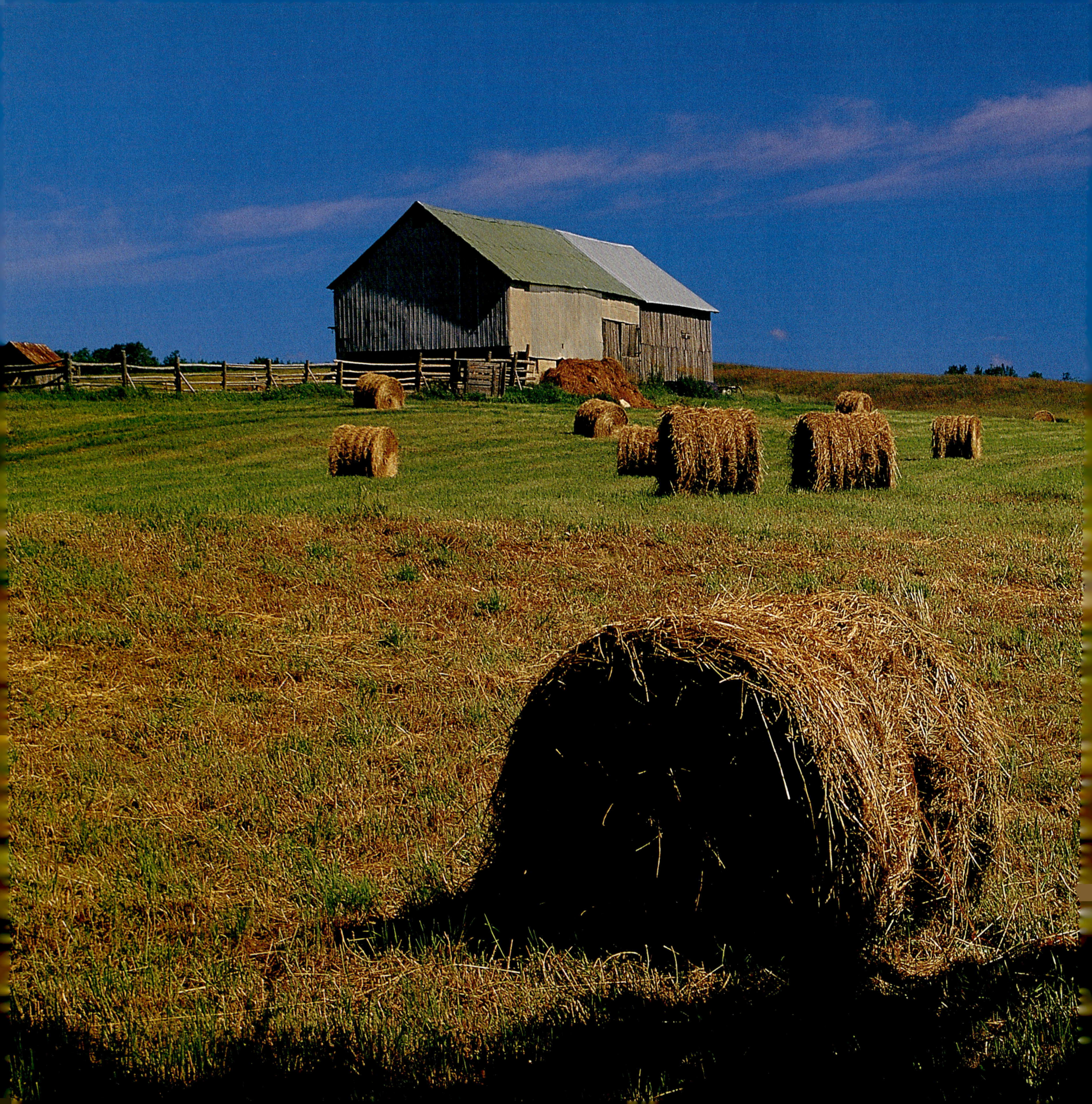

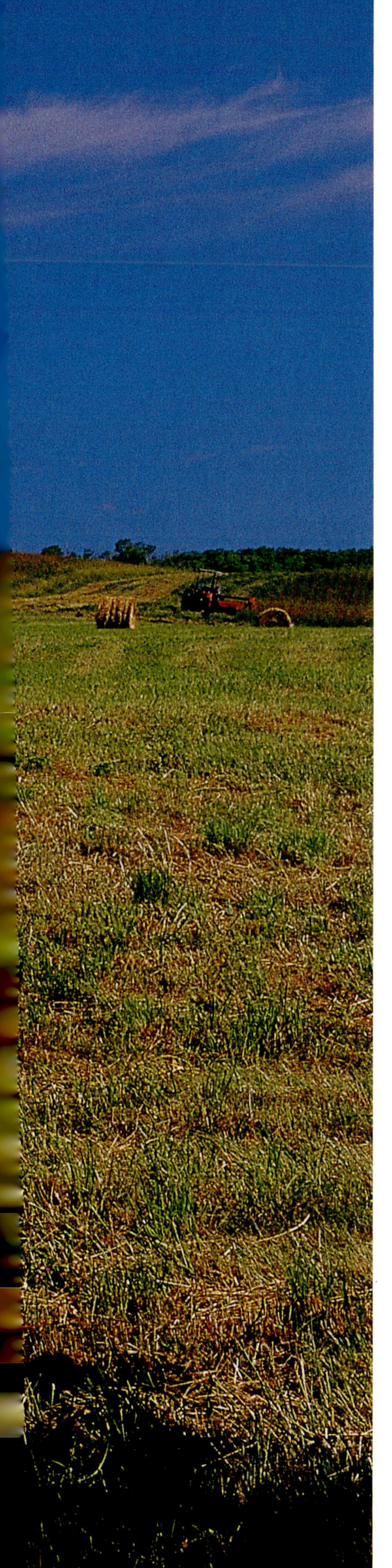

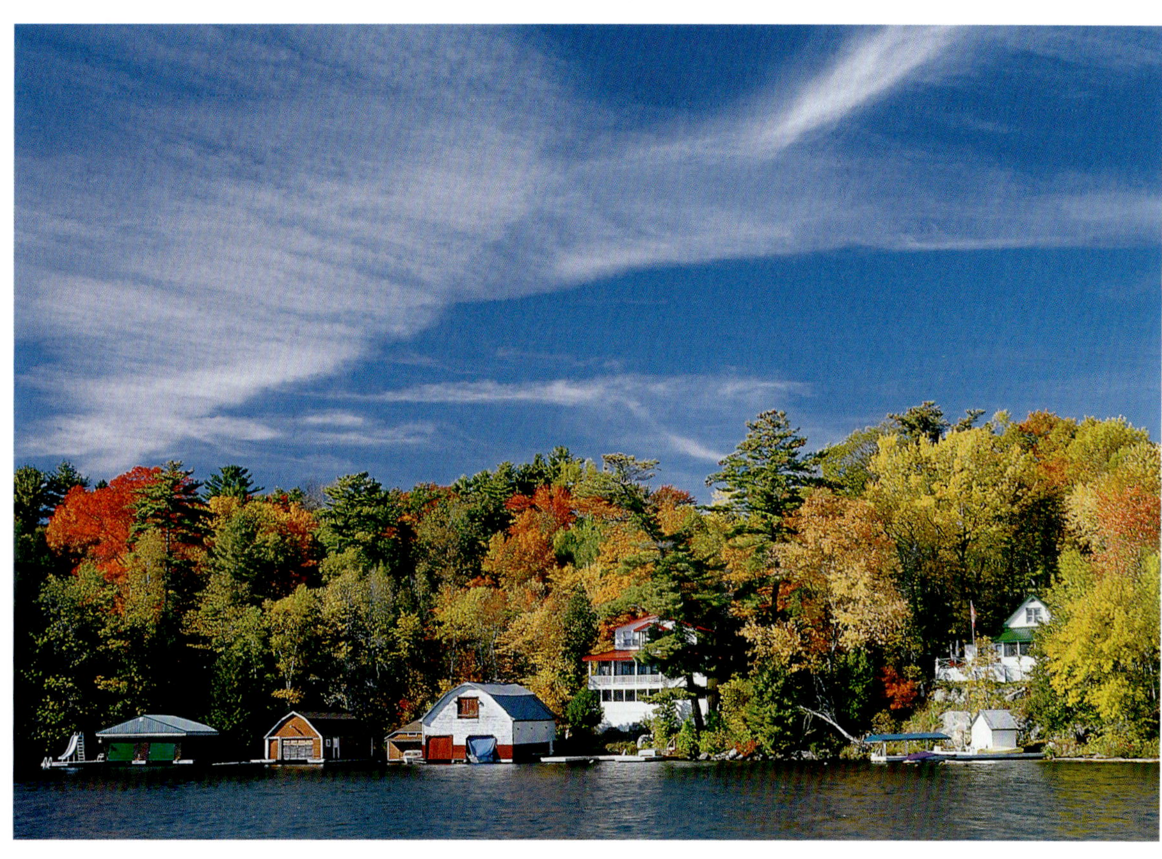

Lake Rosseau is just one of 1,600 lakes in the Muskokas. About 50,000 full-time residents call the region home, but the population triples with summer residents and visitors.

Manitoulin Island is named for the Great Spirit of the Ojibwa people, Gitchi Manitou. A piece of the Niagara Escarpment that juts from the waters of Lake Huron, this is the largest freshwater island in the world.

Summer days in the Muskokas end with scenes like this one—pines silhouetted by the resplendent sunset. The maples in the mixed forests here turn brilliant red with approaching autumn, making fall almost as popular as summer.

FACING PAGE—
Cleveland House has been welcoming visitors to the Lake Rosseau since carpenter, boat builder, and innkeeper Charles Minett constructed a log cabin and hotel here in the late 1800s. The 121-hectare (300-acre) resort offers tennis, pools, golf, barbecues, and more.

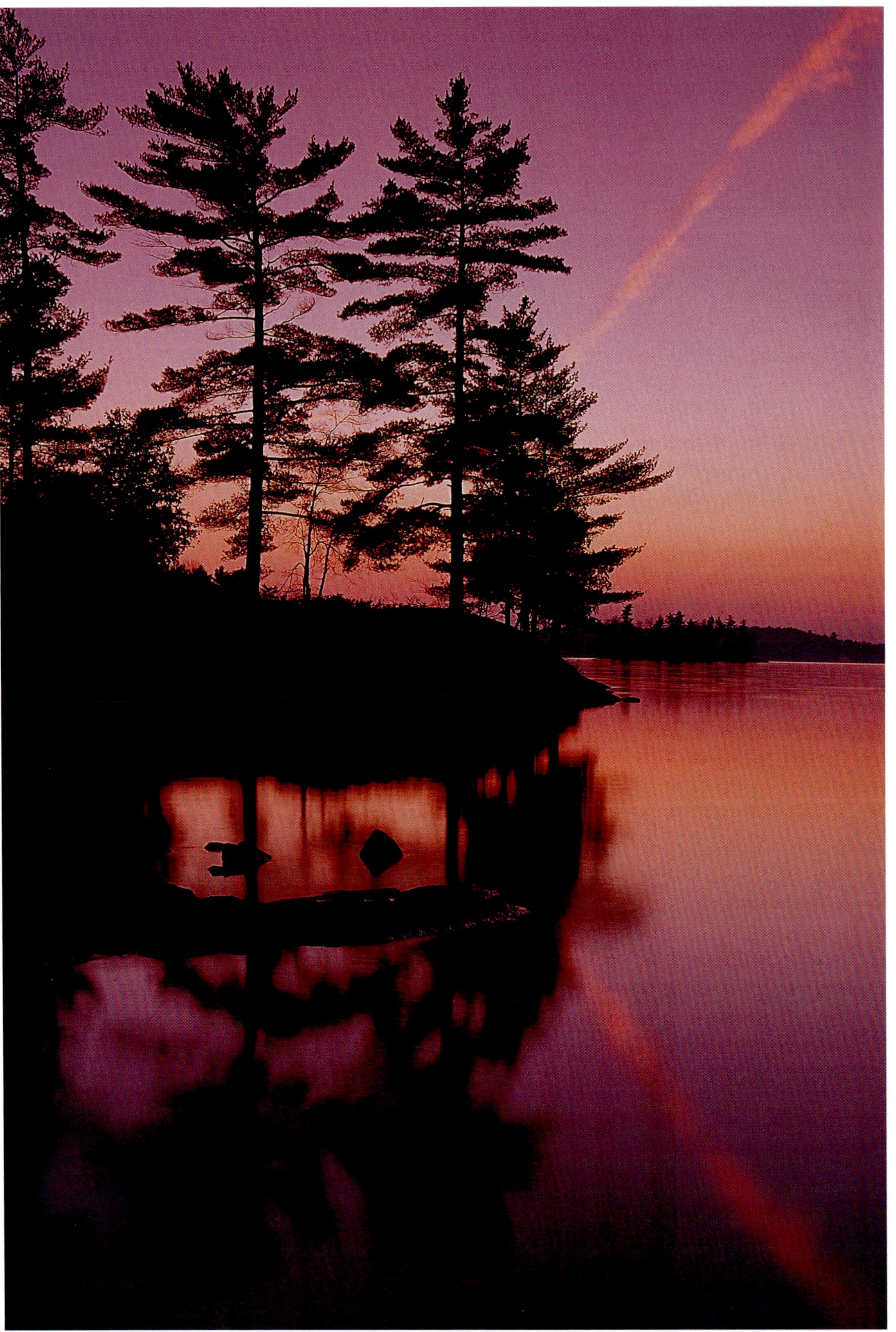

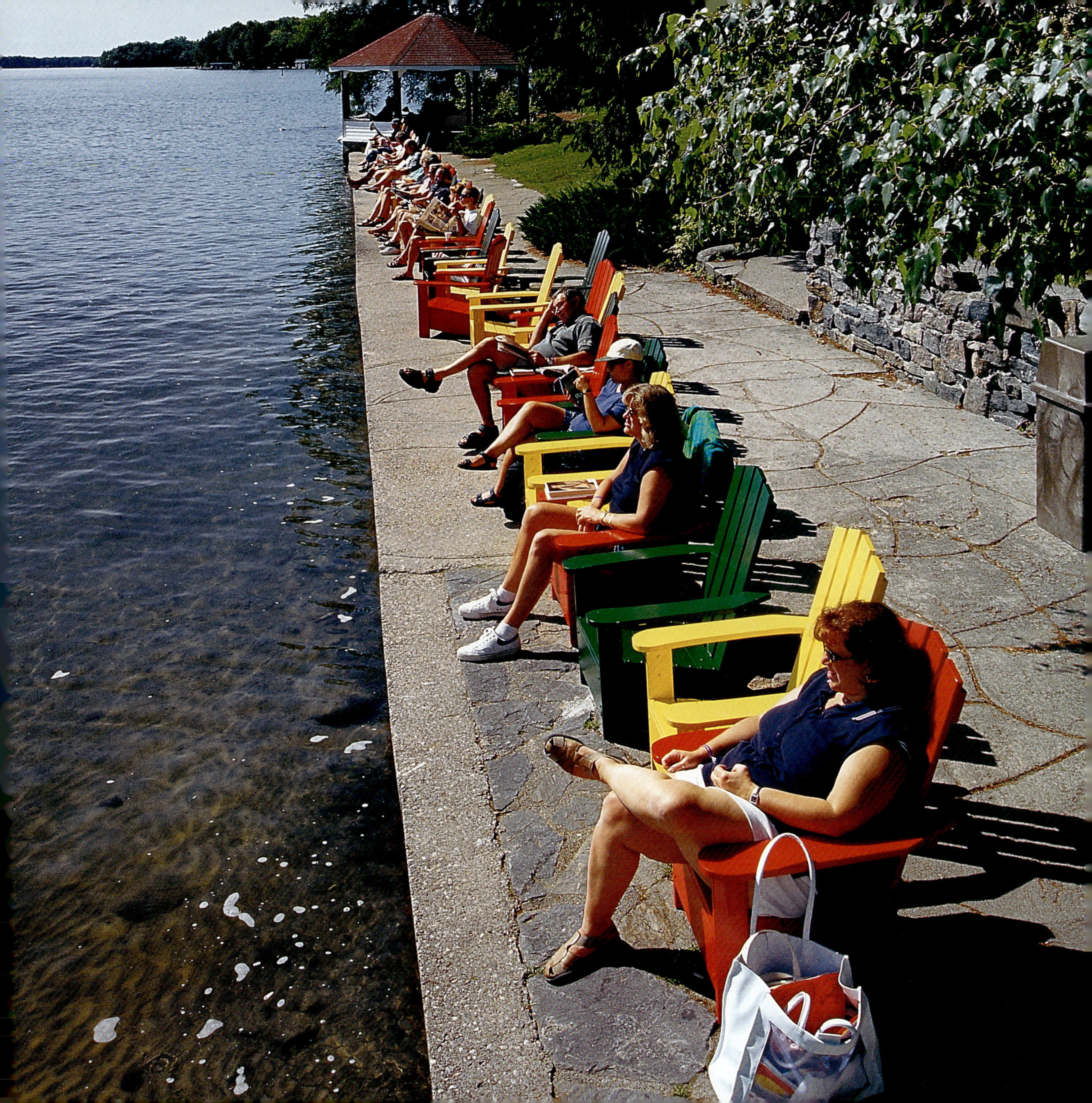

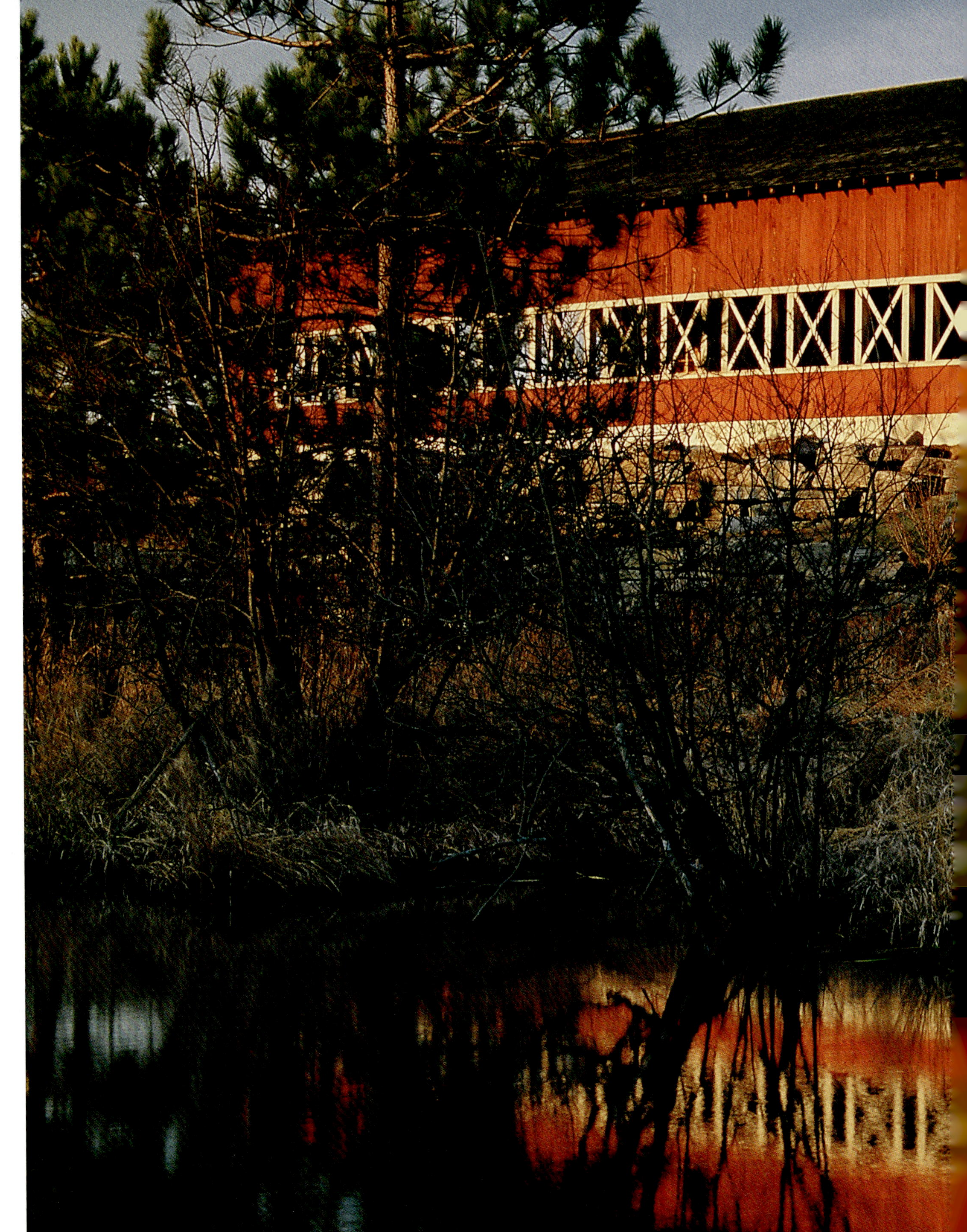

A hiking trail leads past a picturesque covered bridge near Bracebridge. This was one of the early centres of industry in Muskoka—forest stands were easily logged, the nearby waterfalls offered a good supply of power, and fertile soil tempted new settlers.

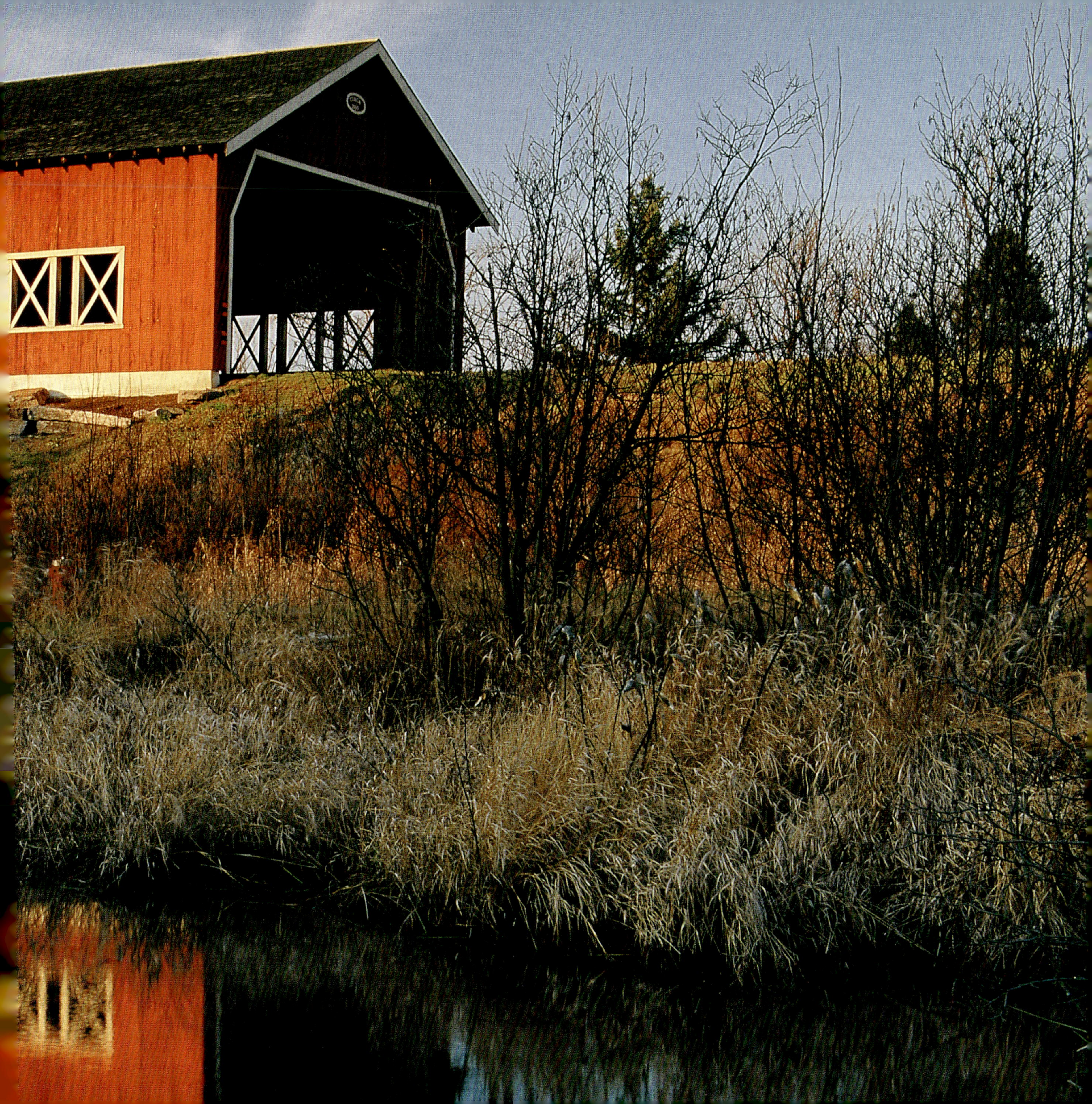

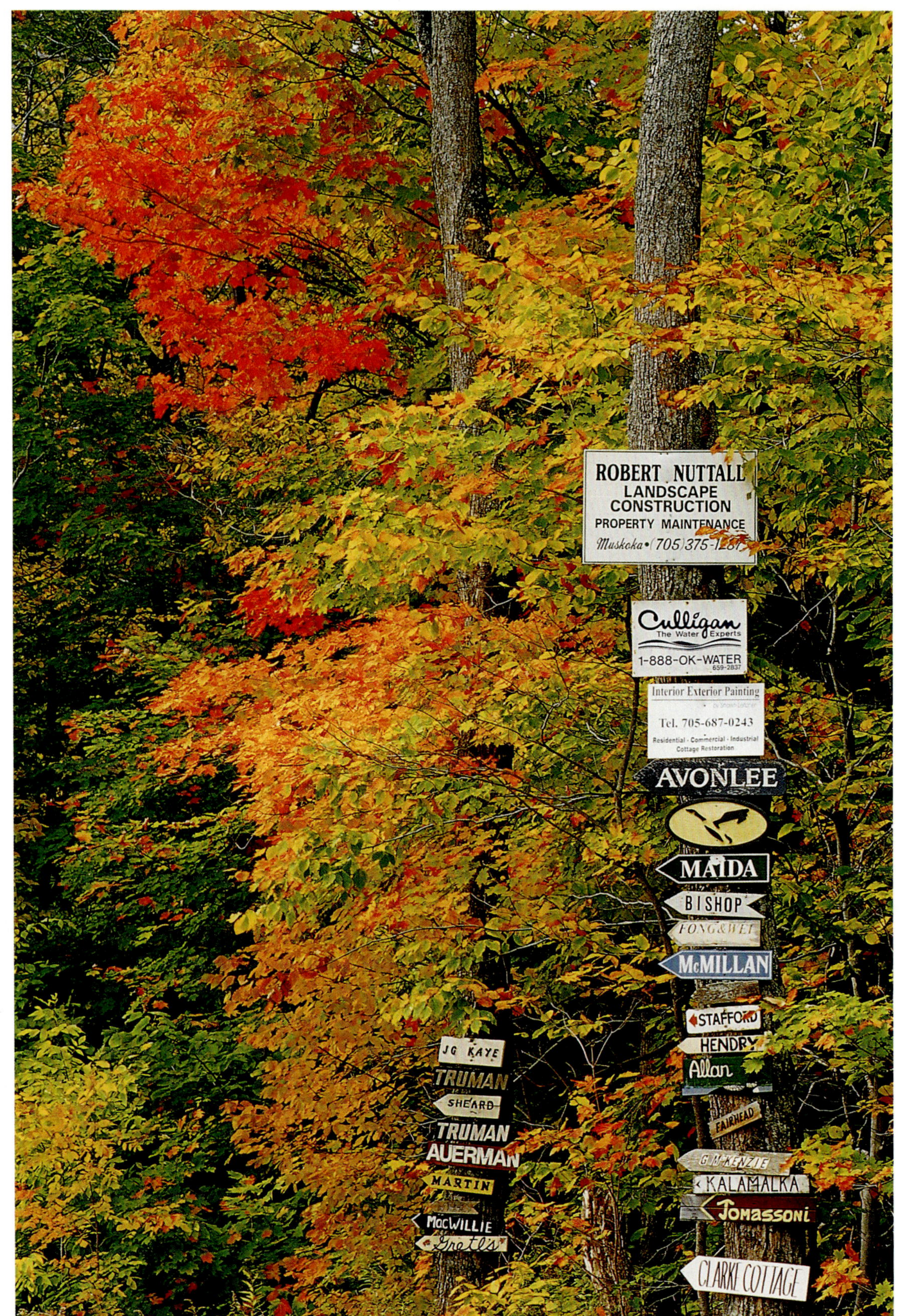

Many of Ontario's cottages are passed from generation to generation. Some of the lakeside property in the Muskokas has been owned by the same families since the region was first settled by European farmers.

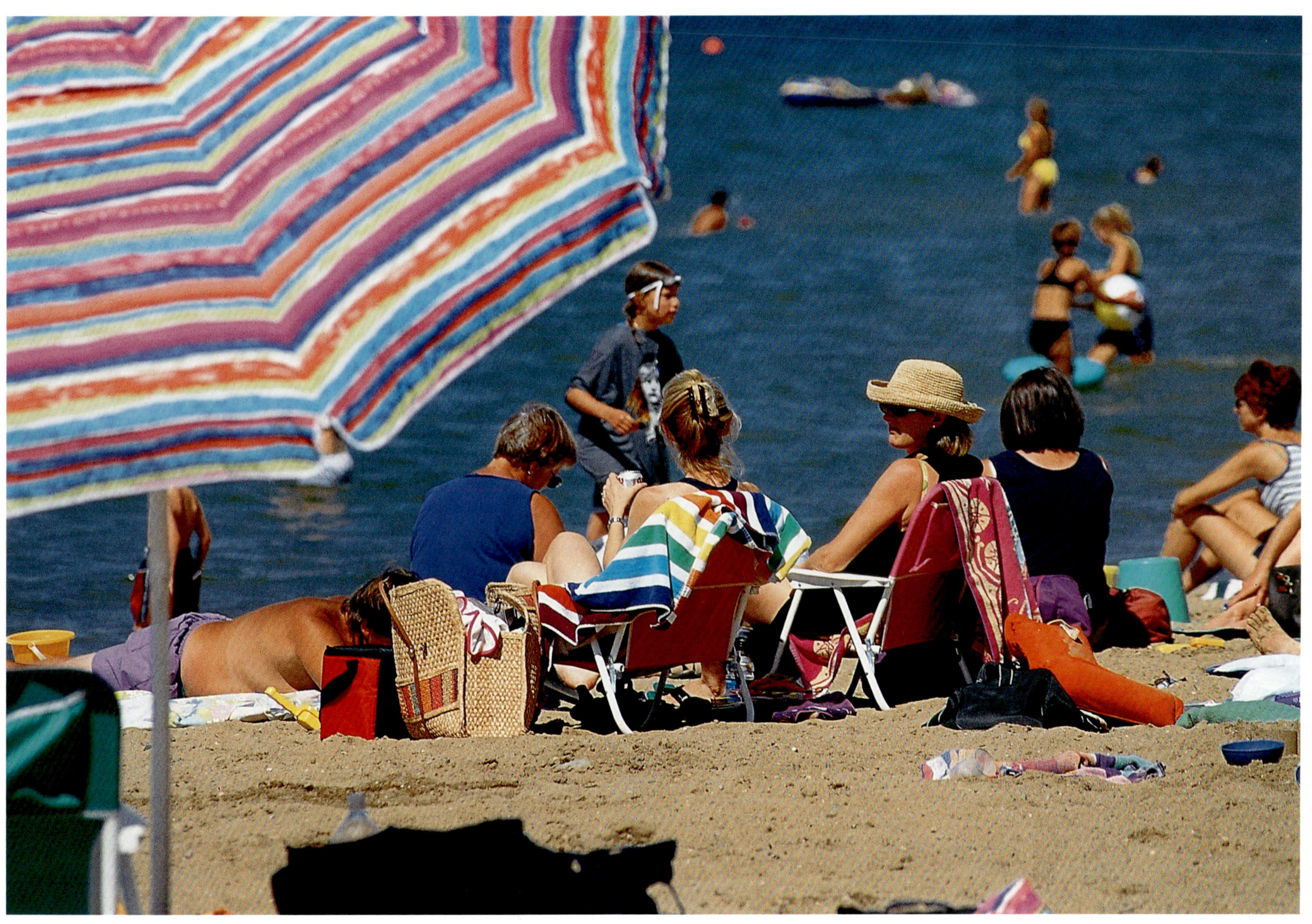

For some, it's a short walk from the cottage to an afternoon of sand and sun. Those looking for a little more adventure can follow the Century Trail, a 100-kilometre (60-mile) cycling tour that leads from the sandy shores of Lake Huron to pine forests and small lakeside towns.

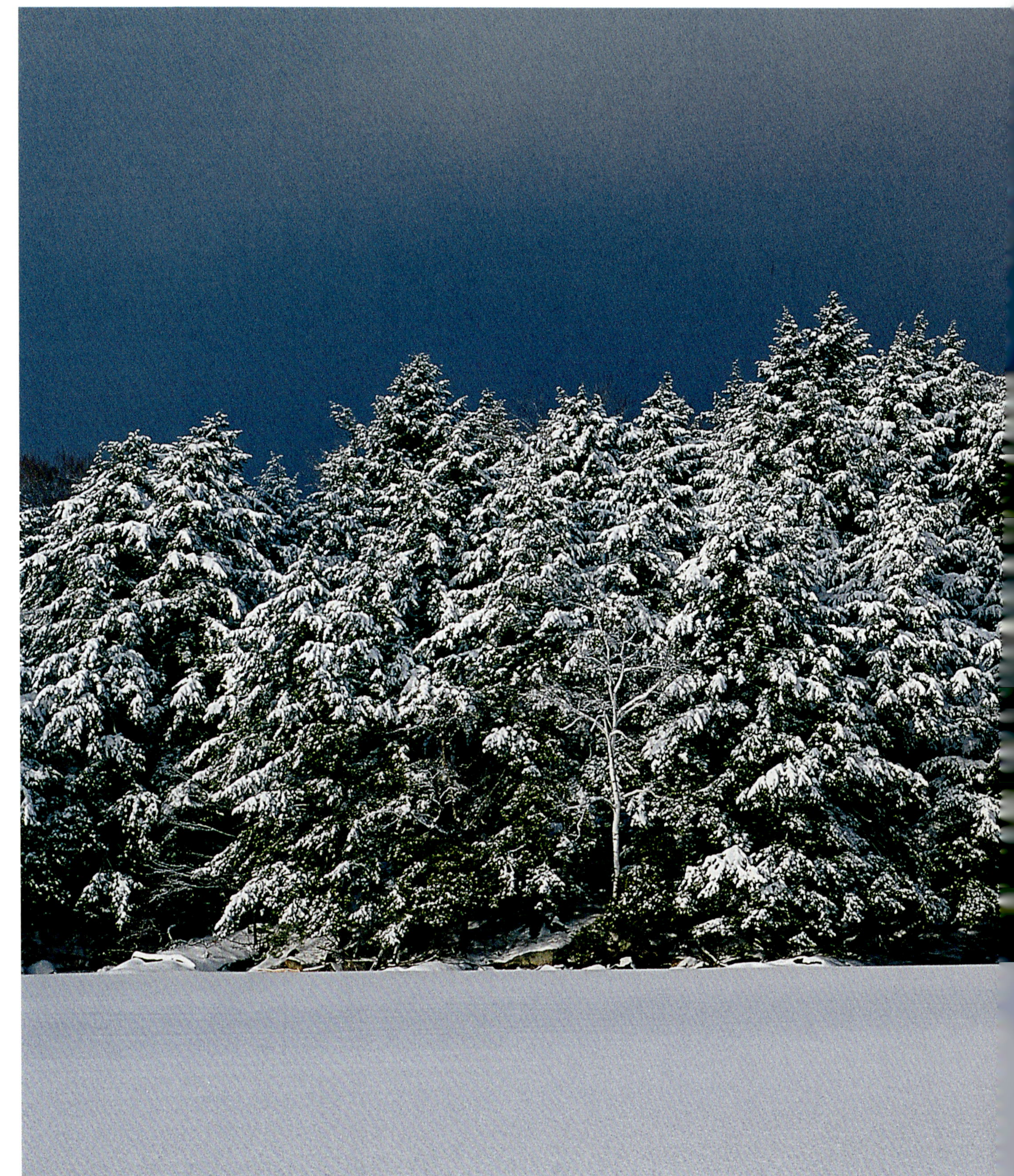

The forests of southern Ontario yielded riches to the French explorers and traders who travelled here in the early 1600s. Etienne Brûlé embarked on a study of the Huron nation's language and trading practices in 1608, and ships laden with furs were sailing for France by the 1630s.

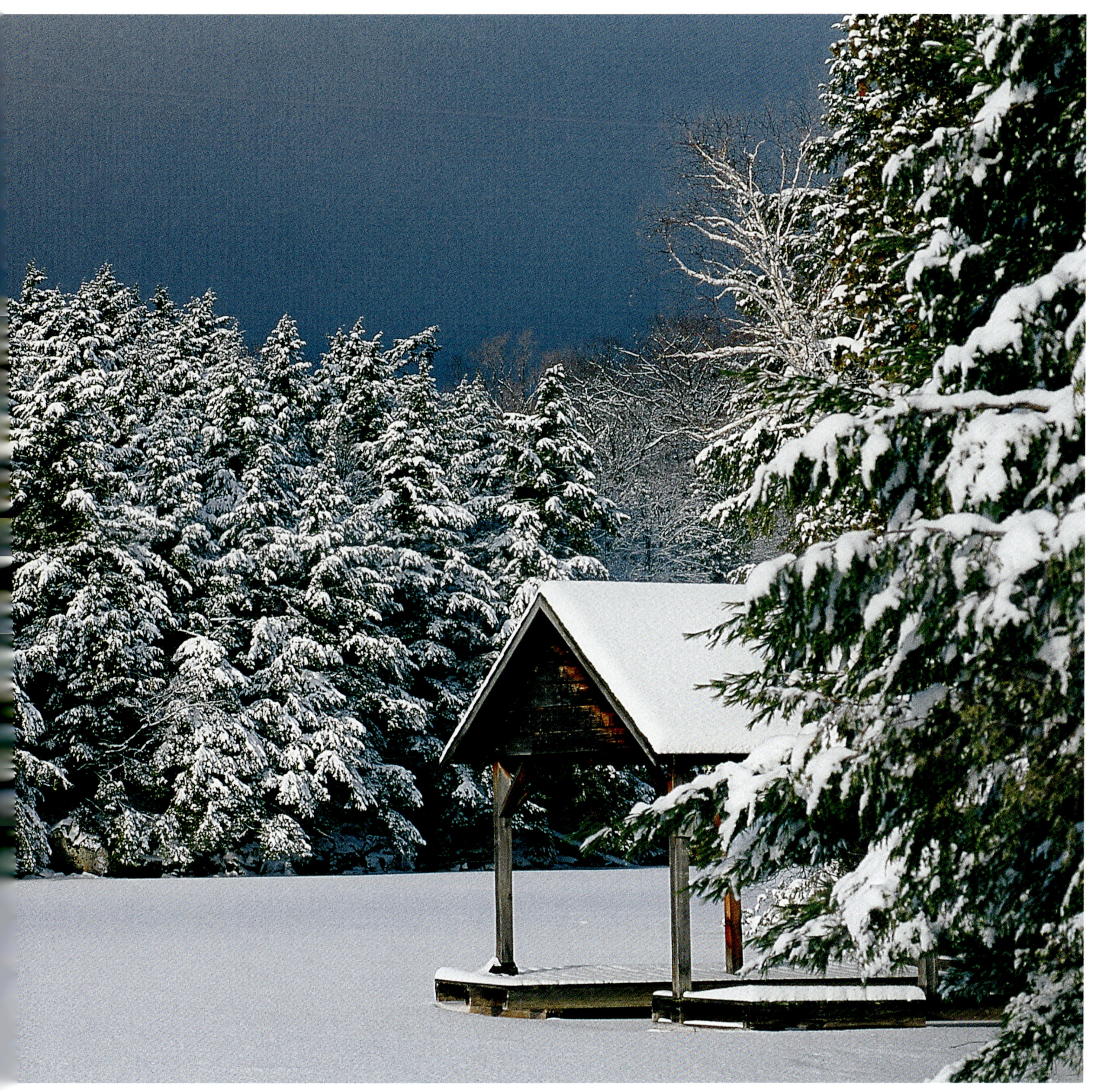

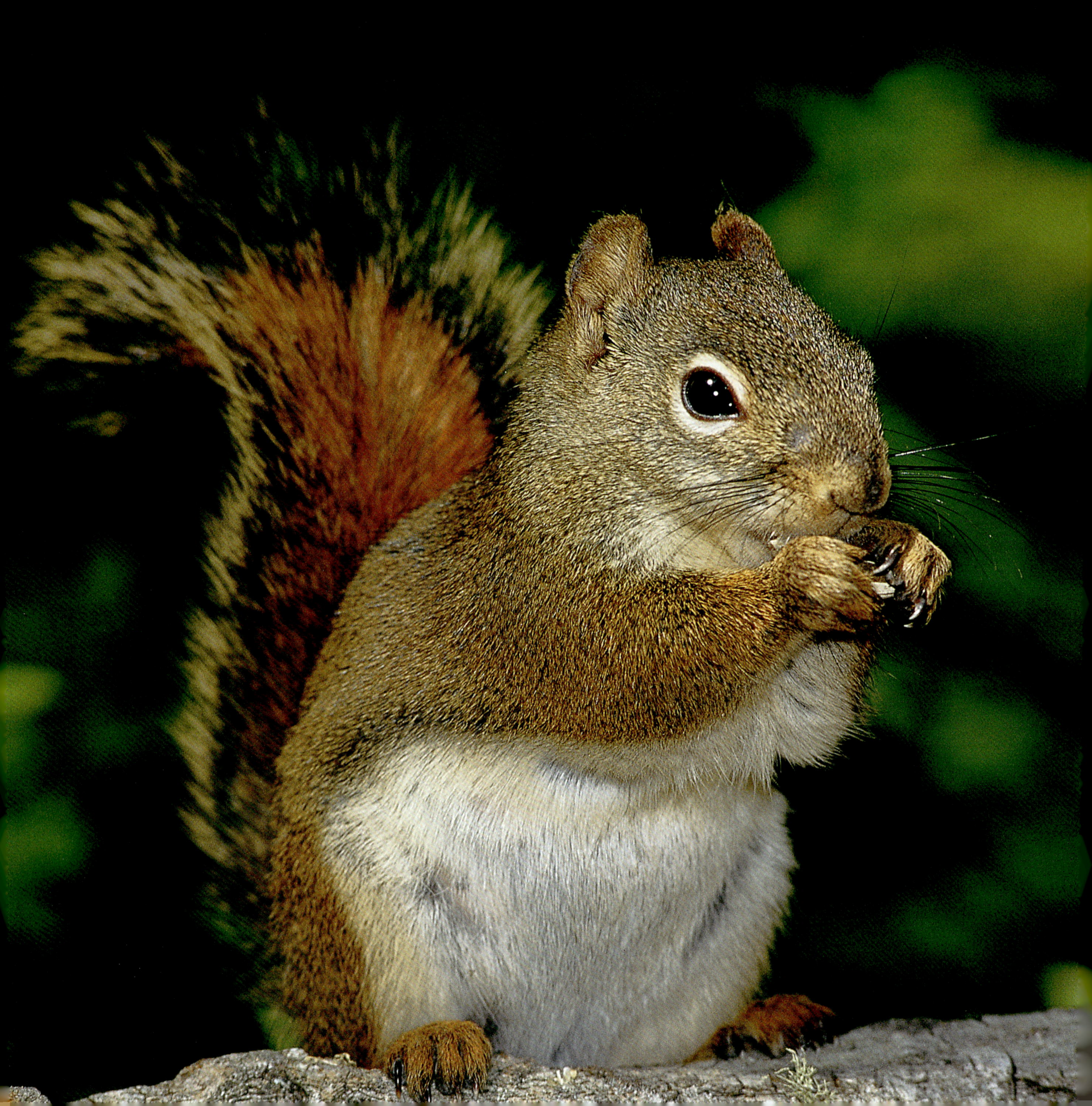

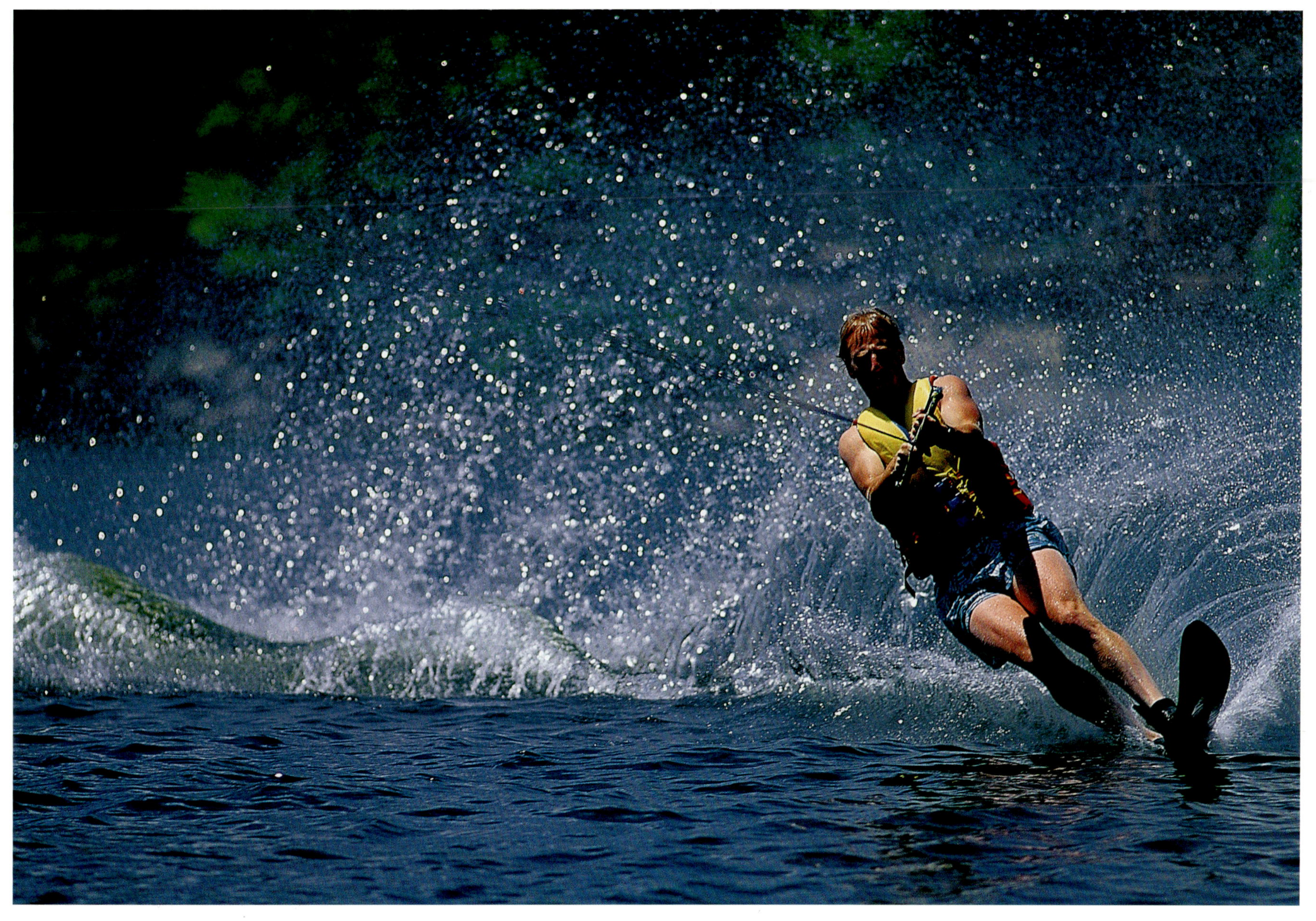

The Muskoka Lakes region is a paradise for water sports. Local dealers sell and rent water skis and wakeboards, while hard-core enthusiasts ski barefoot at local competitions.

The bushy tail of the American red squirrel acts as a rudder, helping it steer and balance as it jumps from branch to branch. The tail also identifies individuals and communicates moods to other squirrels.

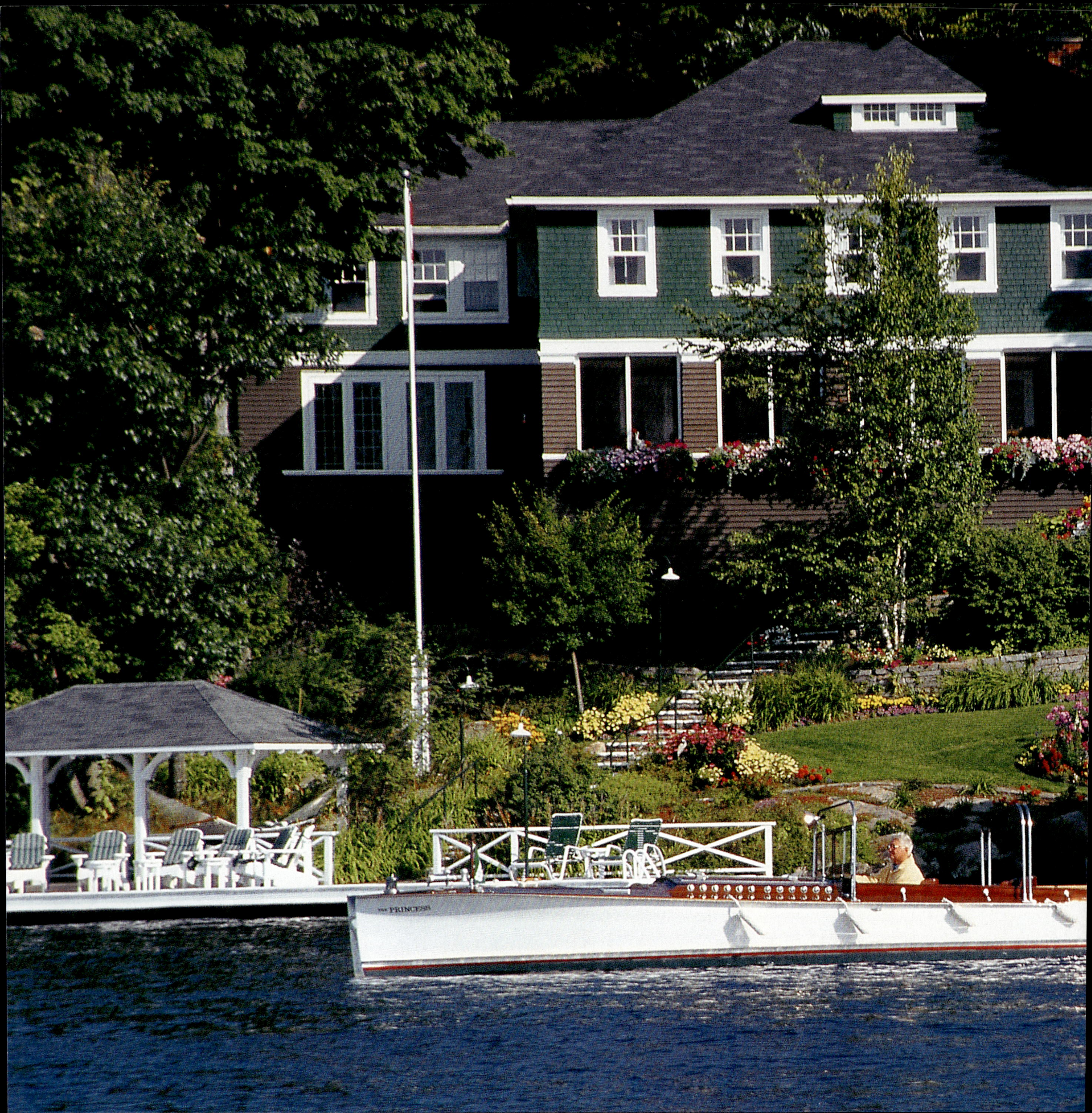
PRINCESS

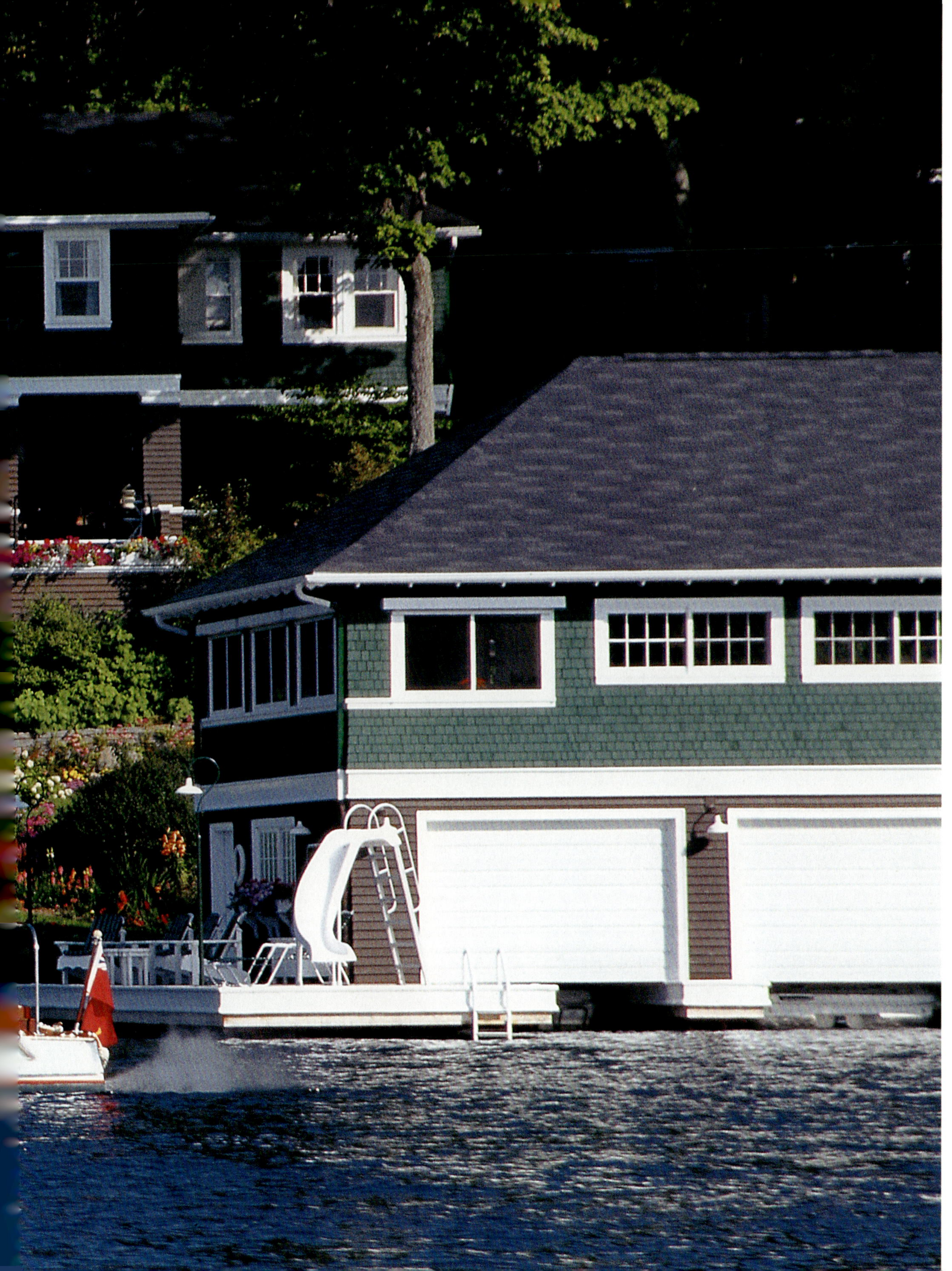

Mid-morning finds the docks and lawns still deserted at this Tondern Island retreat, while vacationers enjoy a lazy brunch indoors.

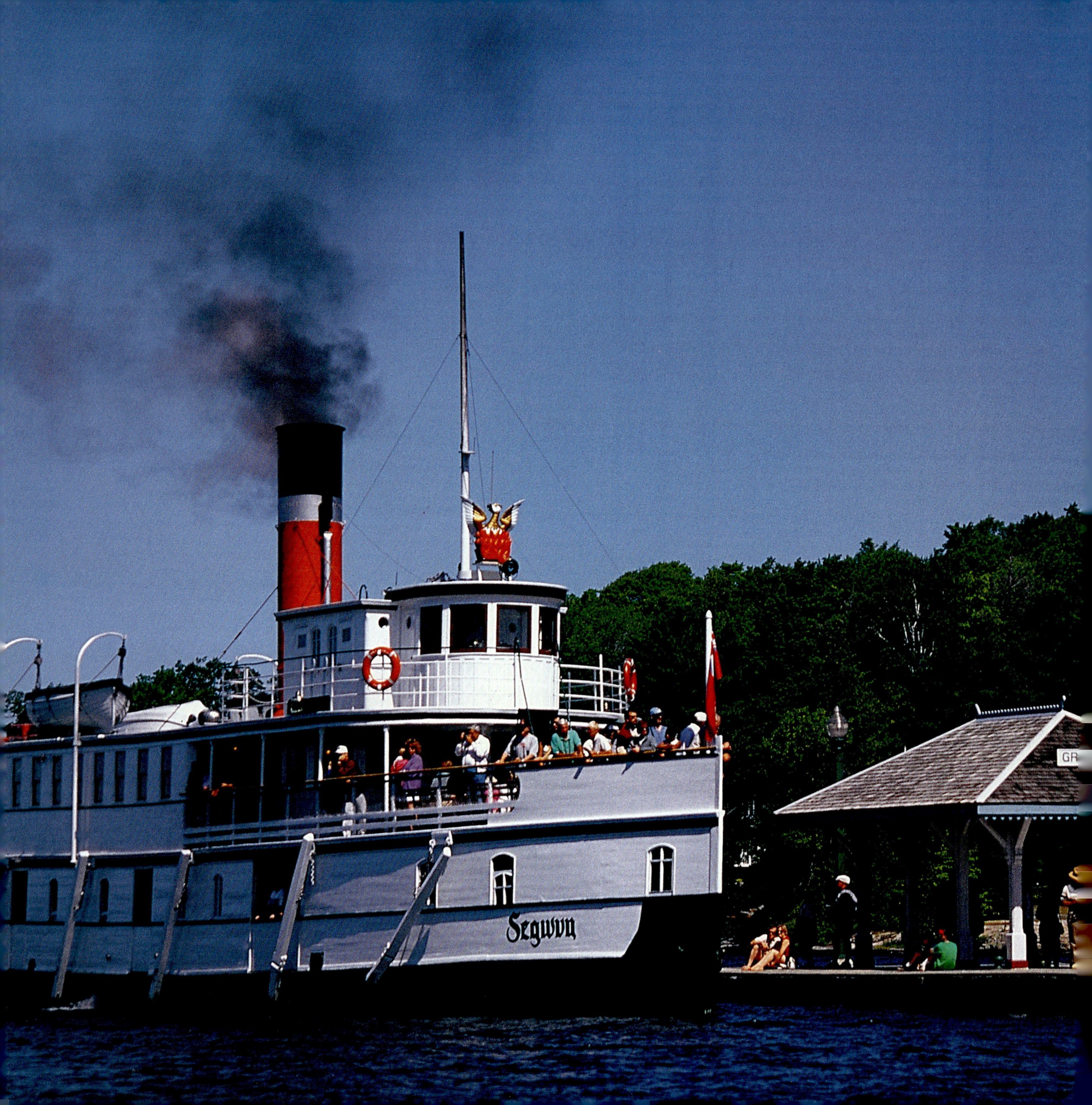
Segwun

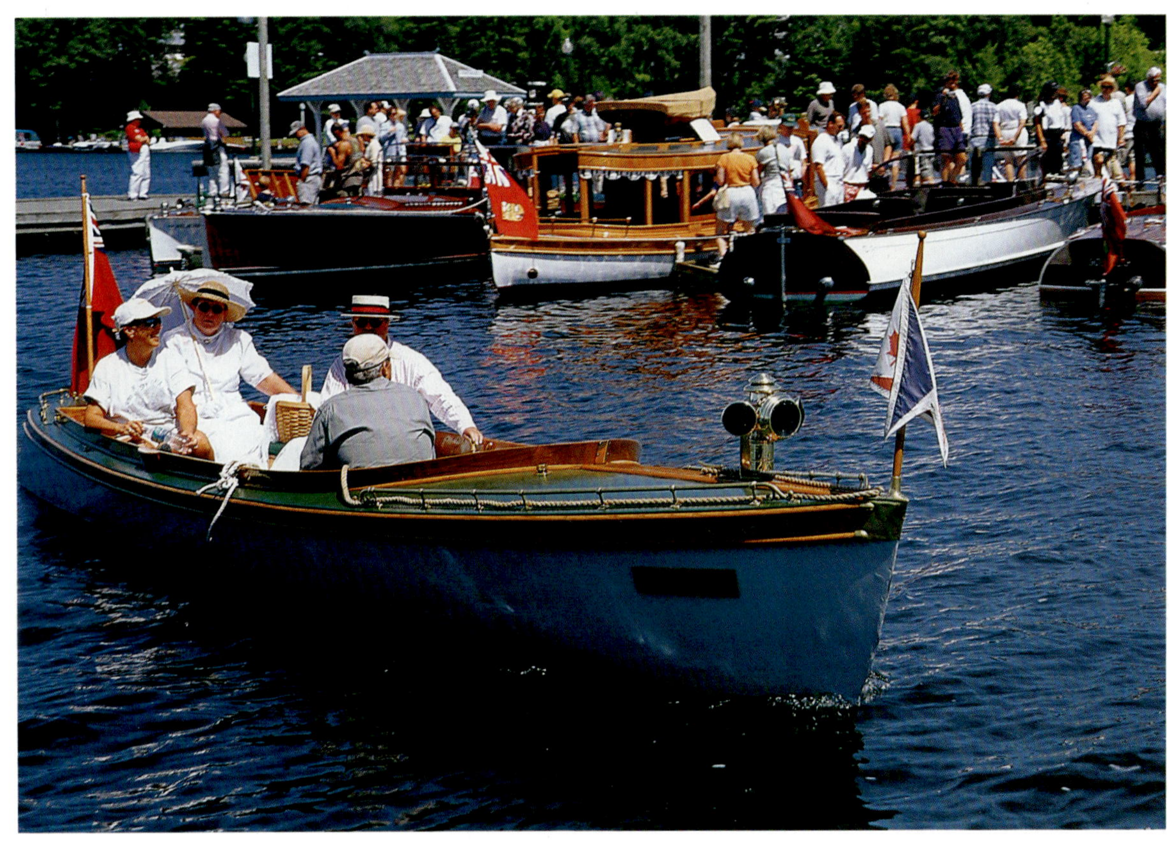

Lake Muskoka is a wonderful place to see some of Ontario's antique wooden boats. A classic boat show has been held here each summer for more than 20 years.

At the tip of Lake Muskoka, the town of Gravenhurst is the birthplace of Dr. Norman Bethune, best known for his medical work in China and for bringing blood-transfusion units to the battlefield.

Raven Lake is just one of dozens within a few kilometres (one or two miles) of the hamlet of Dorset. Kimball, Little Hawk, Oxtongue, Grandview, and Fairy lakes all await nearby.

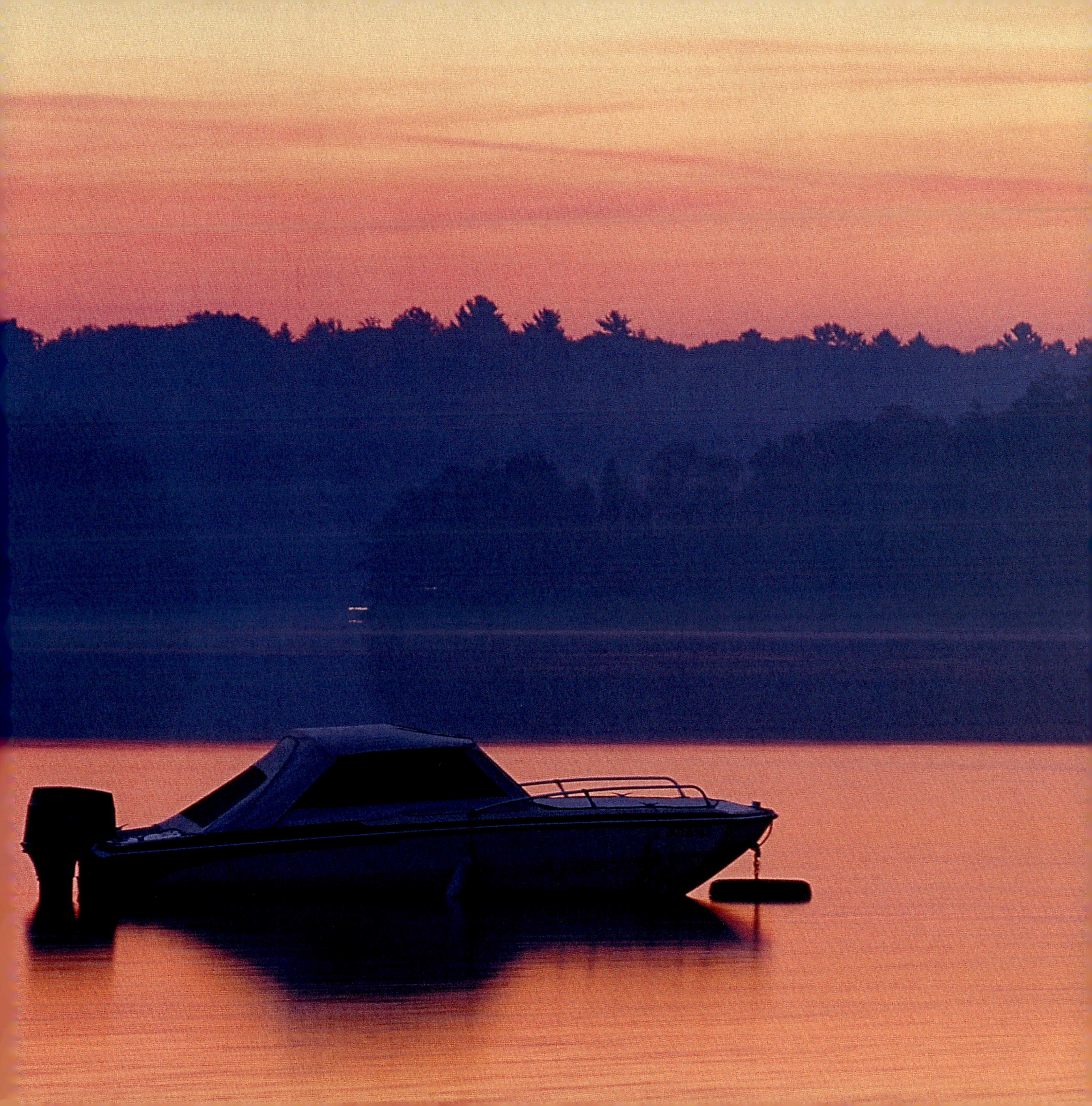

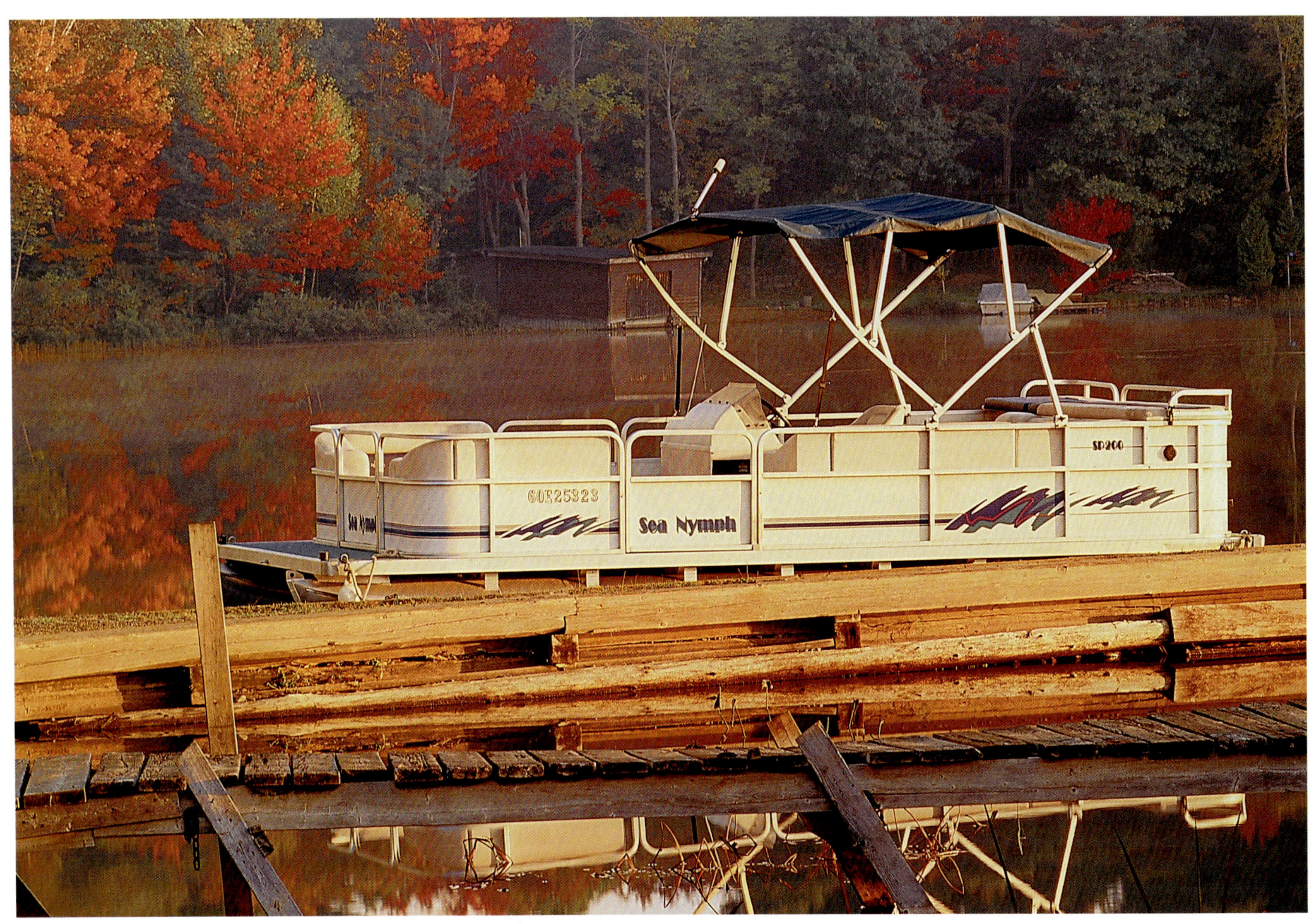

Retirees and artisans who live year-round in the Muskokas have recently discovered a new addition to their ranks. More and more entrepreneurs are running small businesses from their homes in the area.

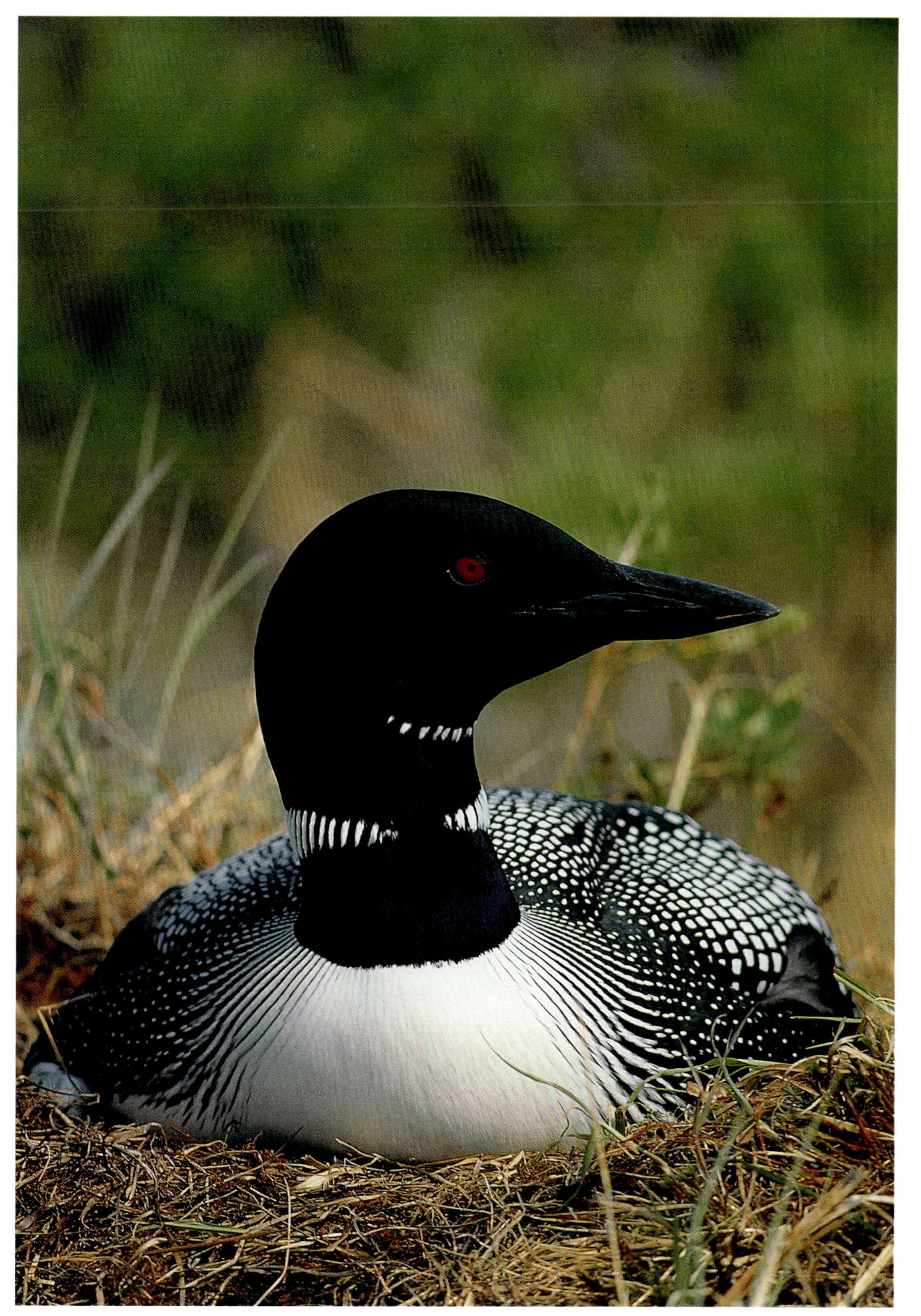

The loon is perfectly designed for diving, with a long, streamlined body and powerful leg muscles far back on its body. As it tracks its underwater prey, the loon opens its wing tips slightly to steer. The loon's distinctive plaintive call can be heard at night.

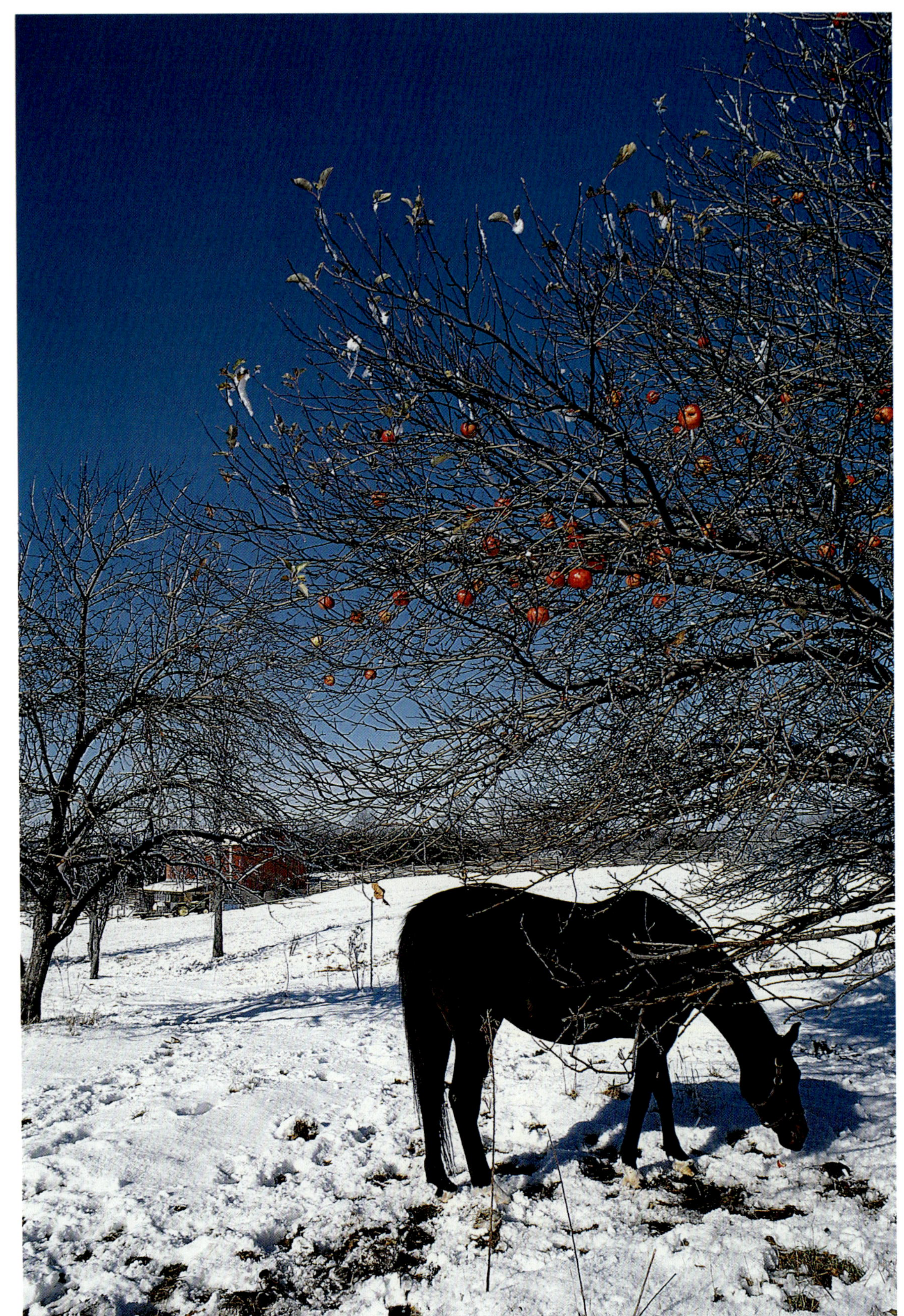

Scattered throughout southern Ontario are hobby farms with a few animals and expansive gardens spread along quaint fencelines. On a long trip to the cottage, it's a pleasent surprise to find fresh produce or flowers for sale from a front drive.

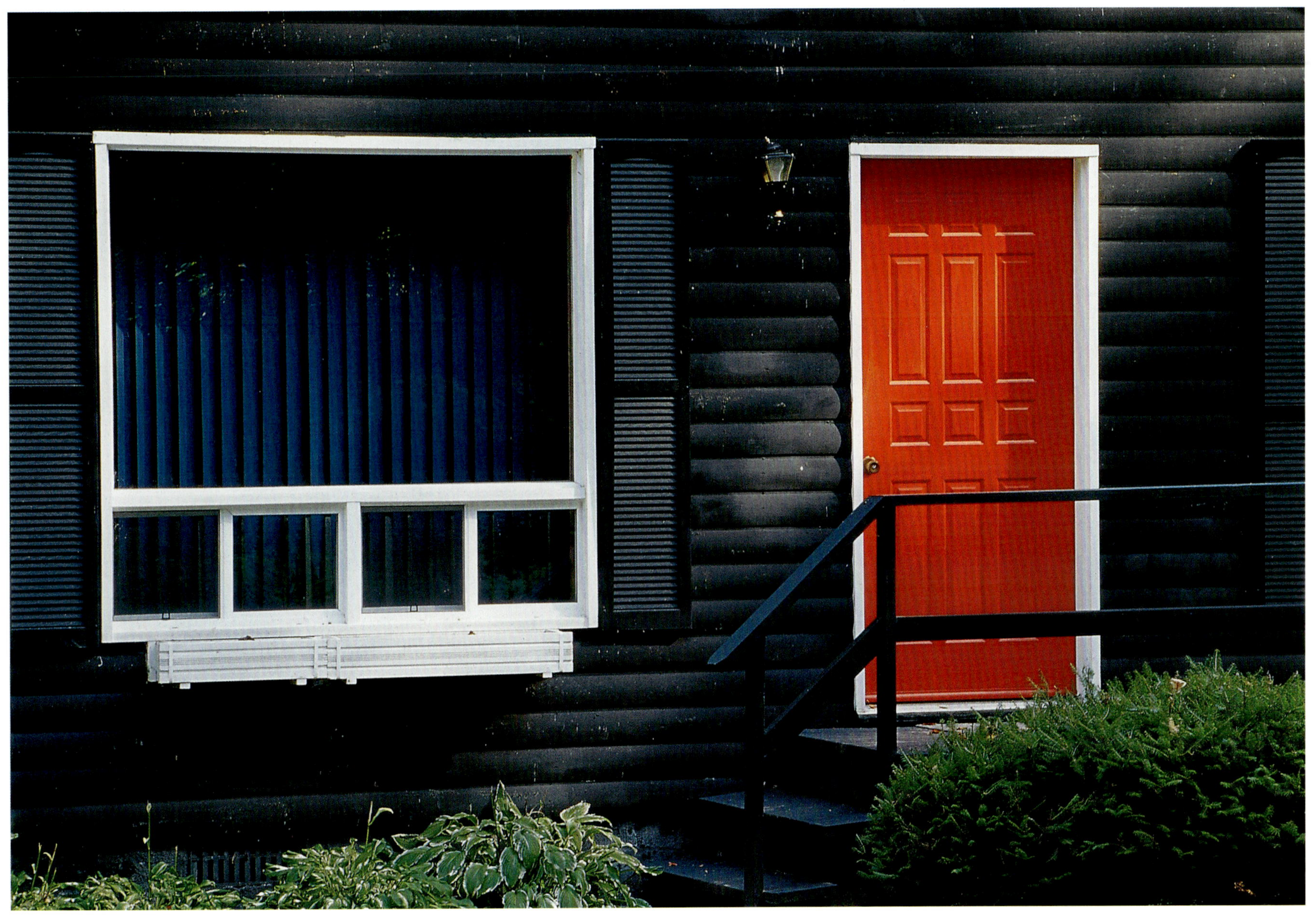

The *crème de la crème* of cottage owners can be found at Lake of Bays and its posh Bigwin Island. Here, movie stars and moguls find their summer respites.

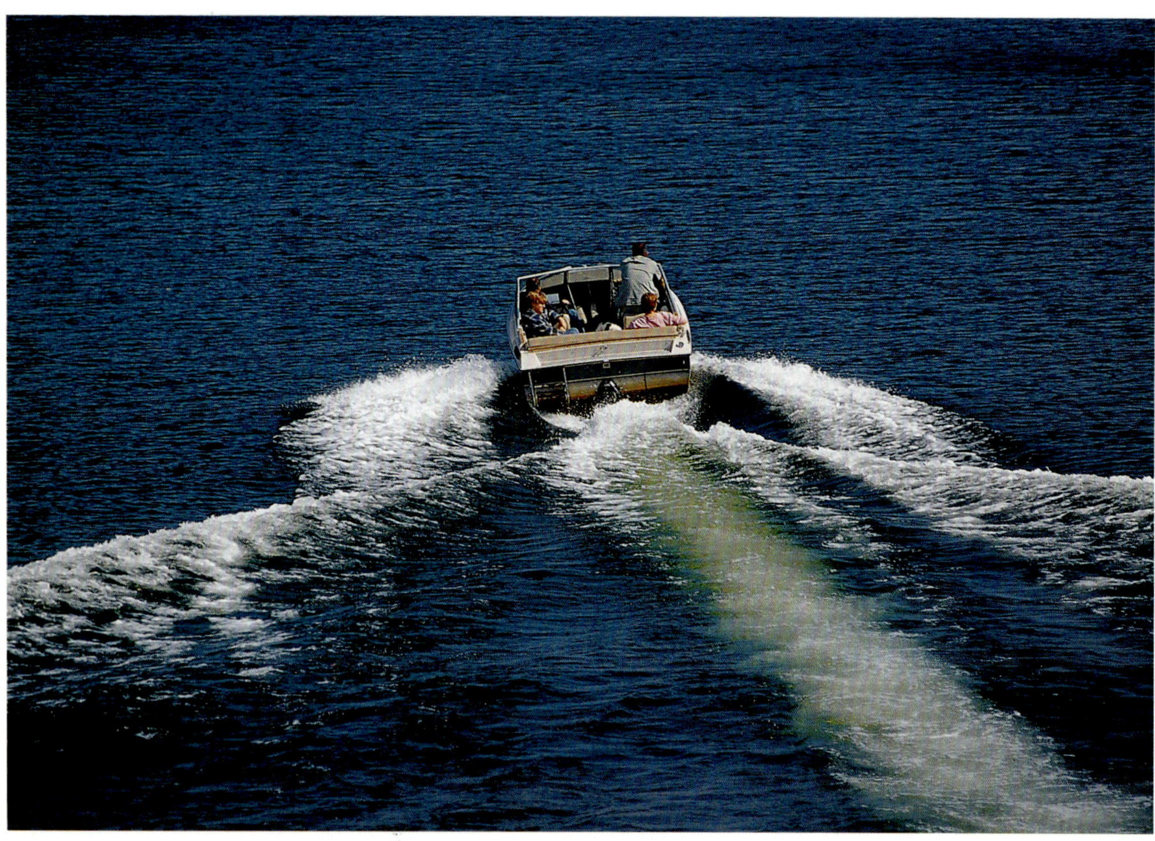

For thousands of cottagers, Dorset serves as home base. Lying on the border between the Muskoka Lakes region and the Haliburton Highlands, the town offers fuel and groceries, quaint cafés and evening entertainment.

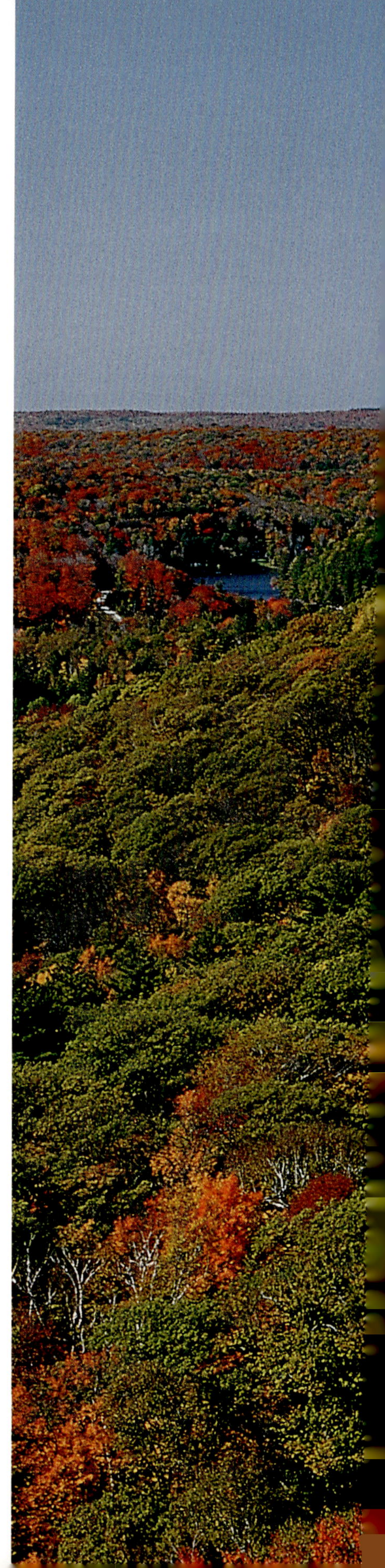

The Haliburton Highlands are a favourite place to see southern Ontario's vibrant fall colours. Bordered by Muskoka and Algonquin Park, the Highlands include more than 20,200 hectares (50,000 acres) of protected woodlands.

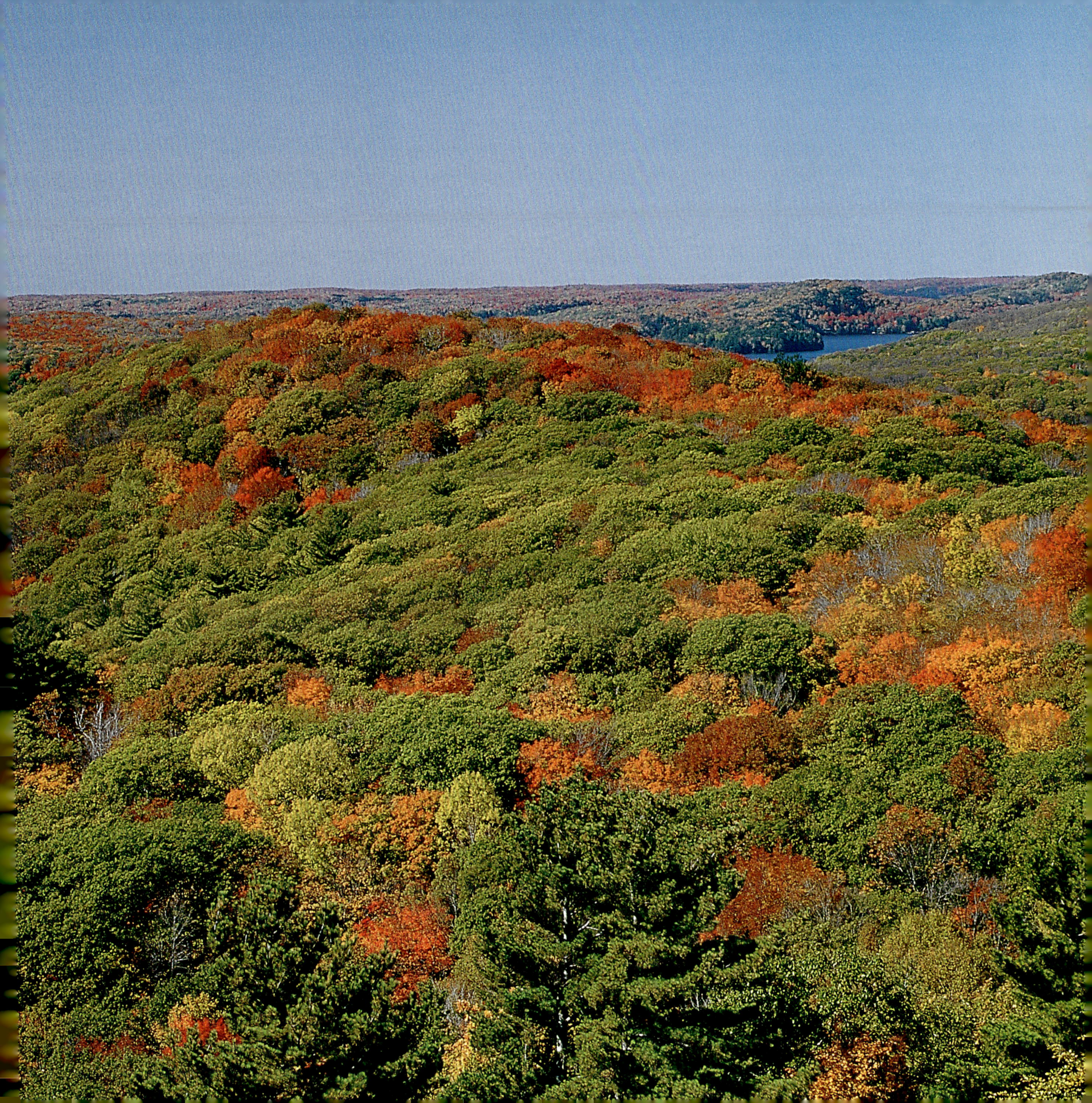

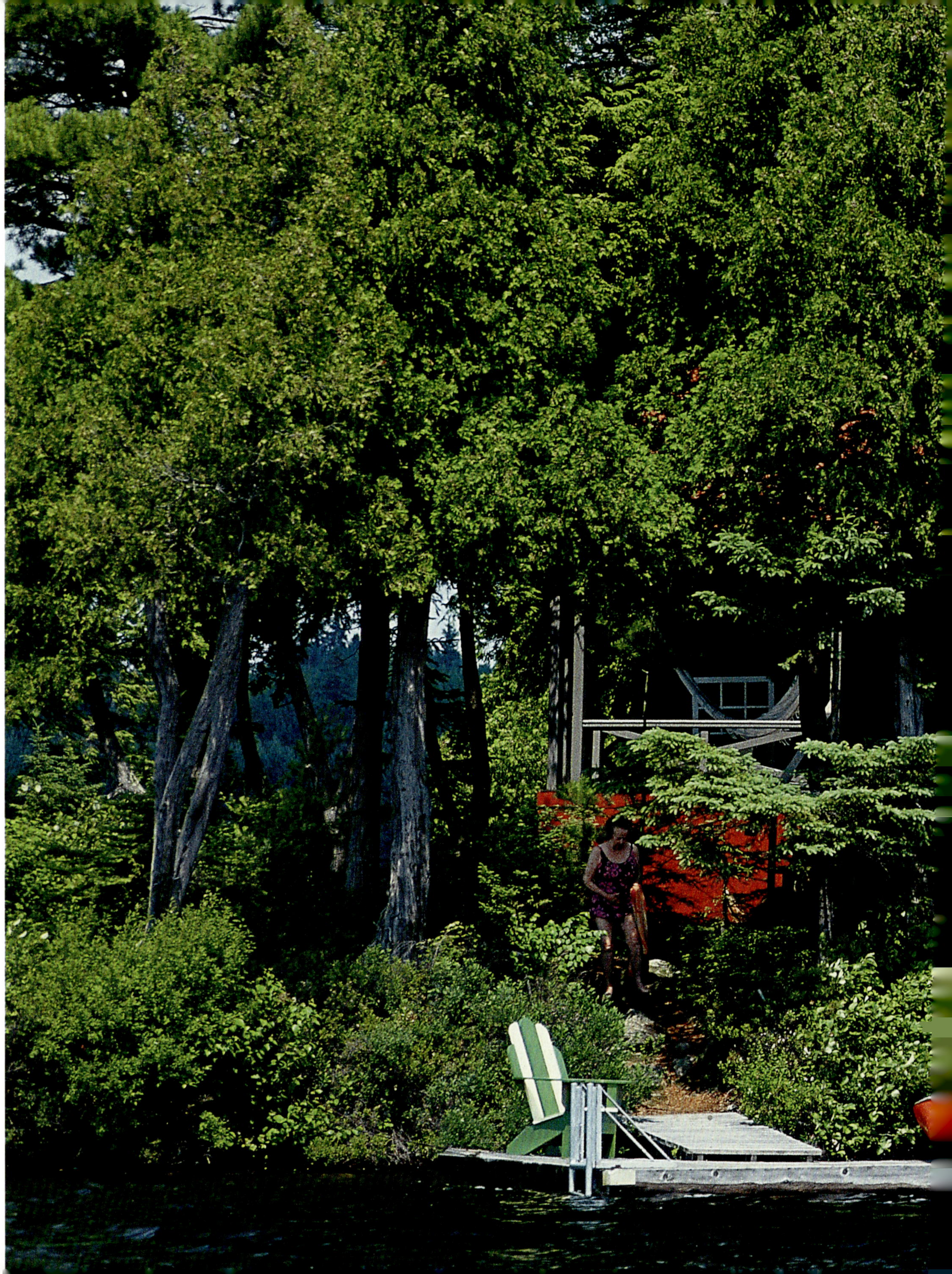

In the 1800s, loggers pushed further and further into the forests, harvesting white pines to fill Britain's booming demand for logs. Preserves such as Algonquin Park helped protect Ontario's flora and fauna.

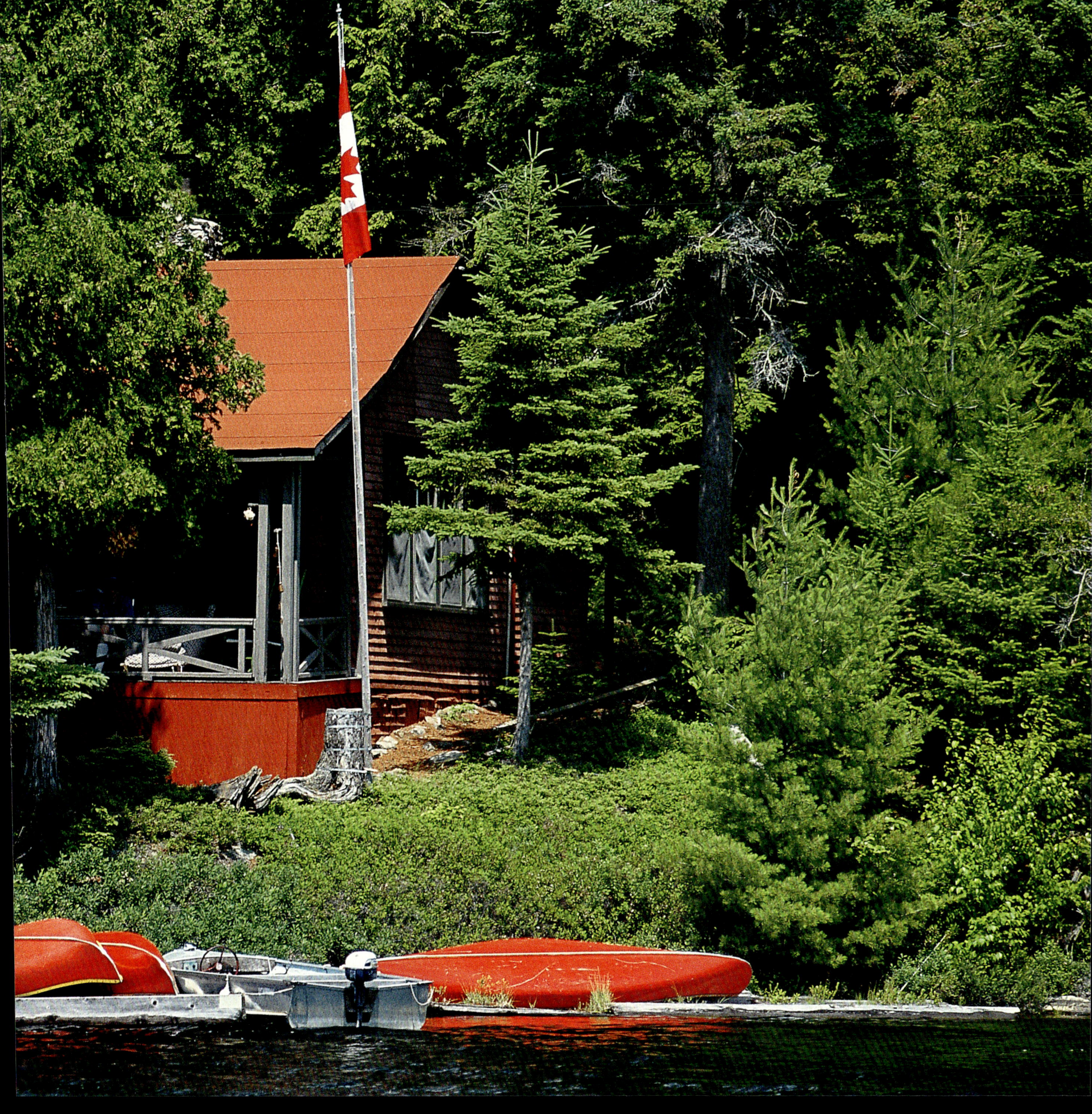

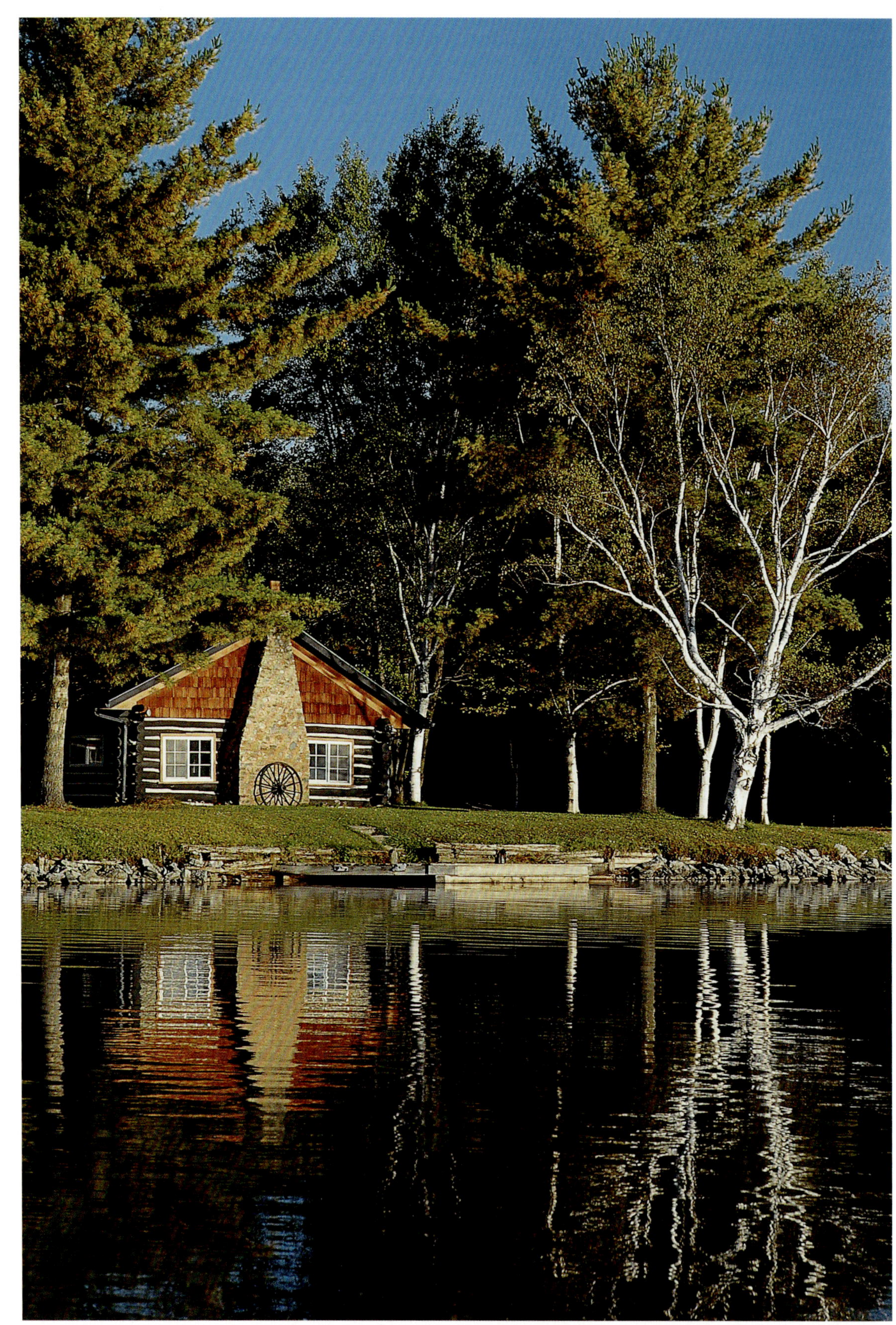

As more galleries and craft shops open in the Muskoka Lakes region, some travellers spend their mornings touring the local studios.

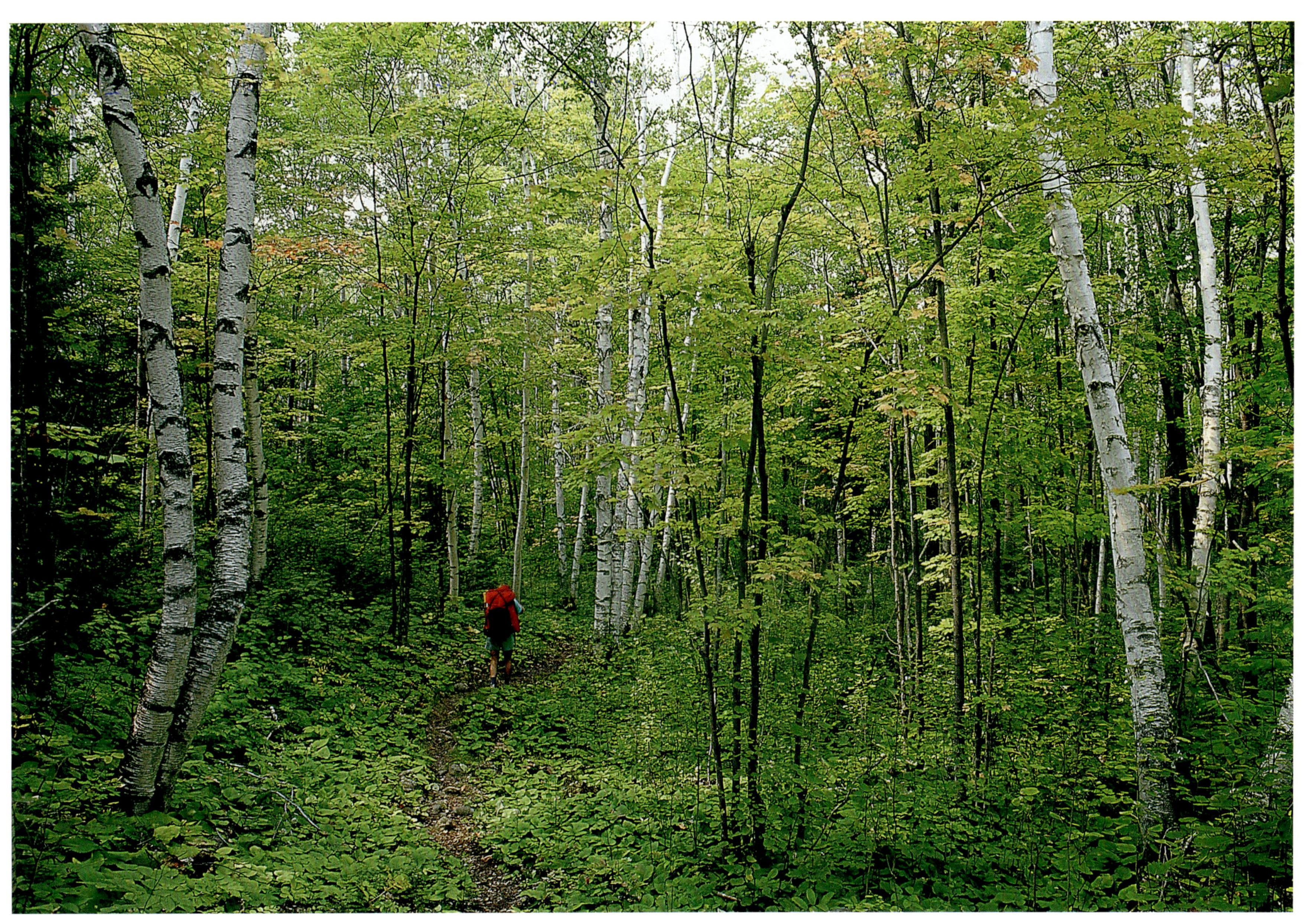

Ontario's first provincial park, Algonquin was established in 1893. Its 7,725 square kilometres (3,000 square miles) are home to a thriving wolf population, seldom glimpsed by the park's human visitors.

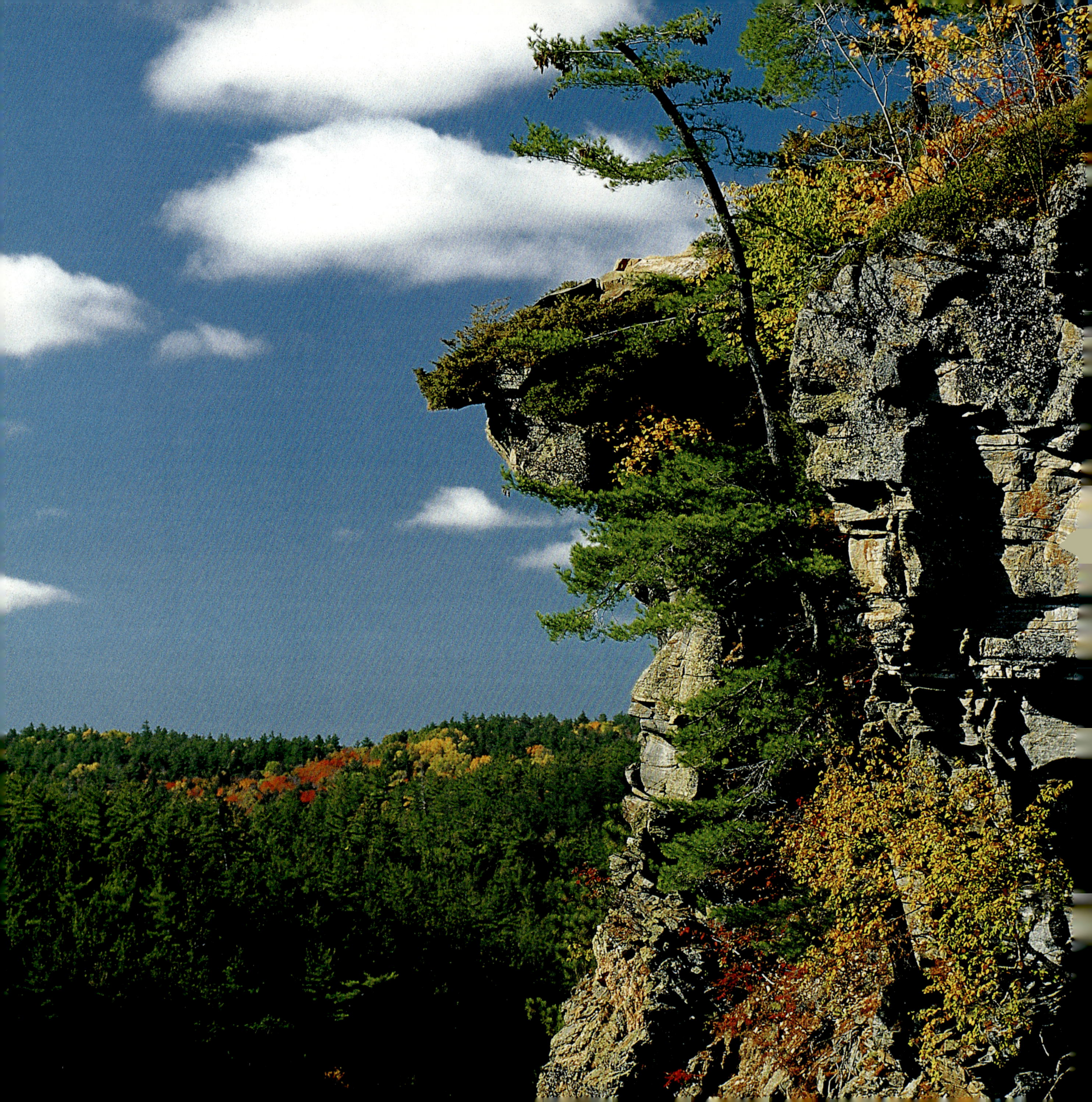

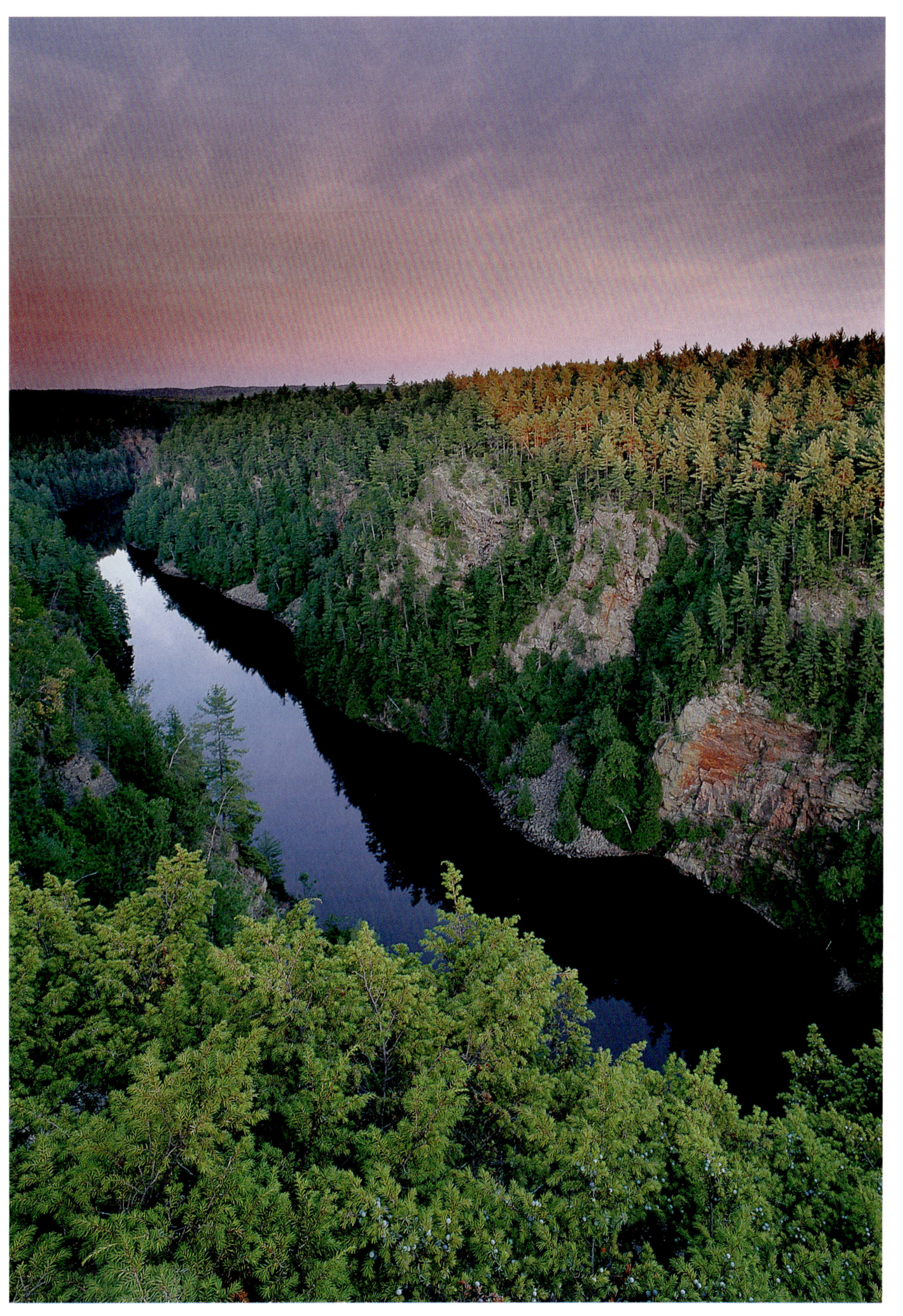

An easy loop trail leads hikers to Algonquin Park's breathtaking Baron Canyon. Twelve other walking trails and three challenging backpacking routes lead to other natural sites within the park.

FACING PAGE—Forty-five mammal species live within the borders of the park, along with more than 260 bird species and 30 kinds of reptiles and amphibians. About 7,000 insect species offer an ever-changing feast to 50 varieties of fish.

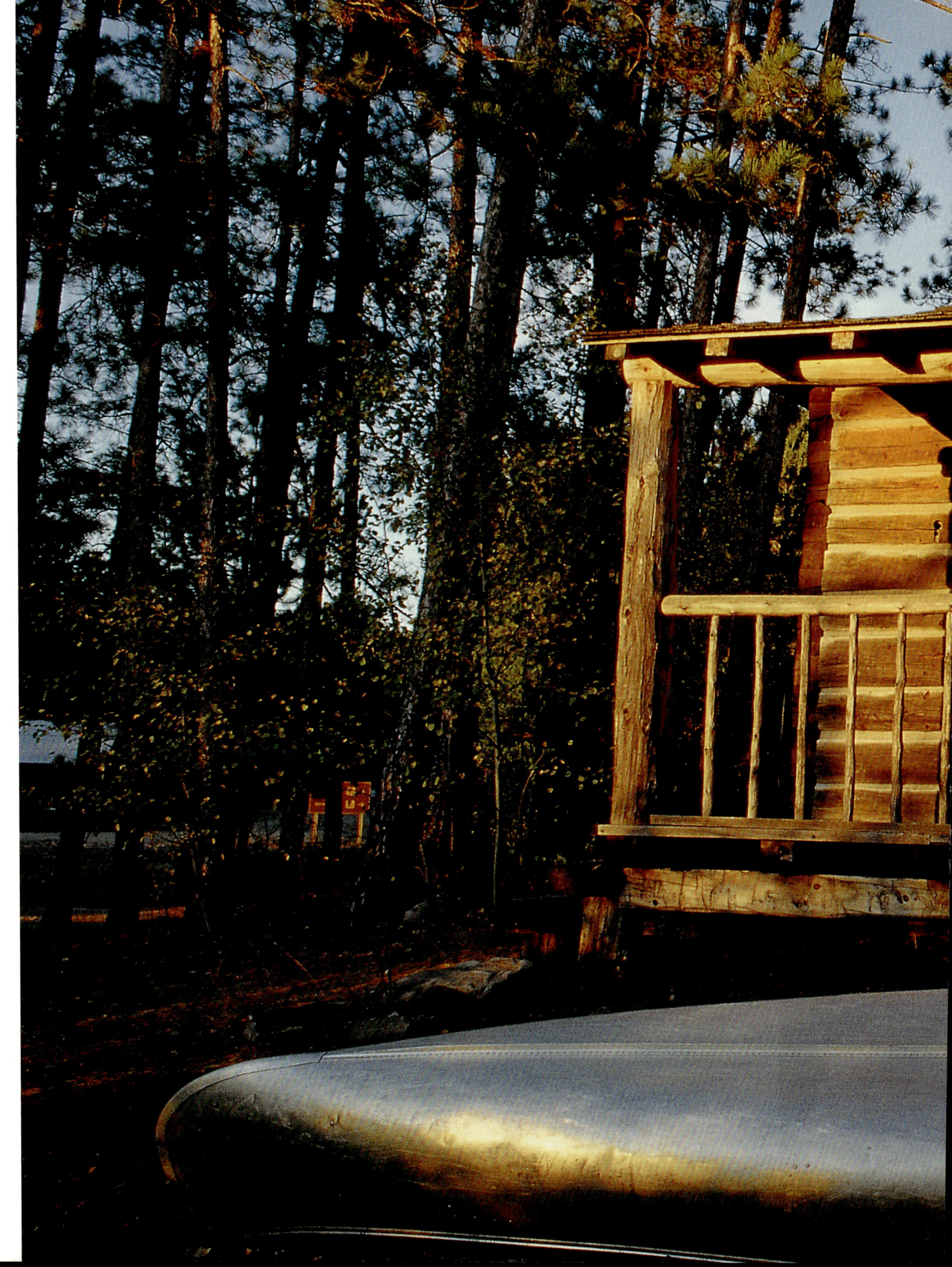

Historic rangers' cabins—some built as early as 1922—dot the backwoods of Algonquin Park. Visitors can reserve some of the remote outposts and experience the solitude felt by those who first patrolled the park.

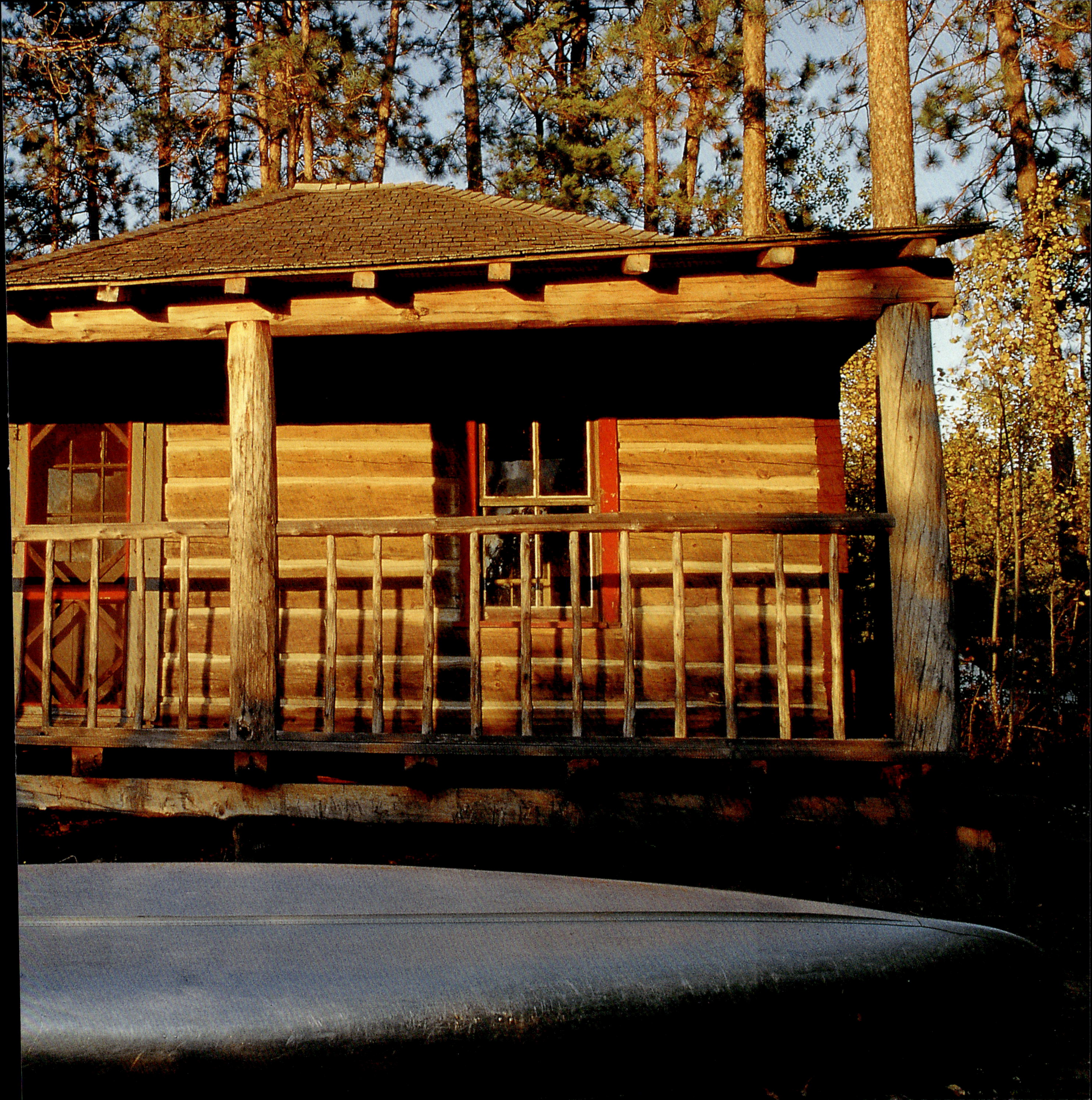

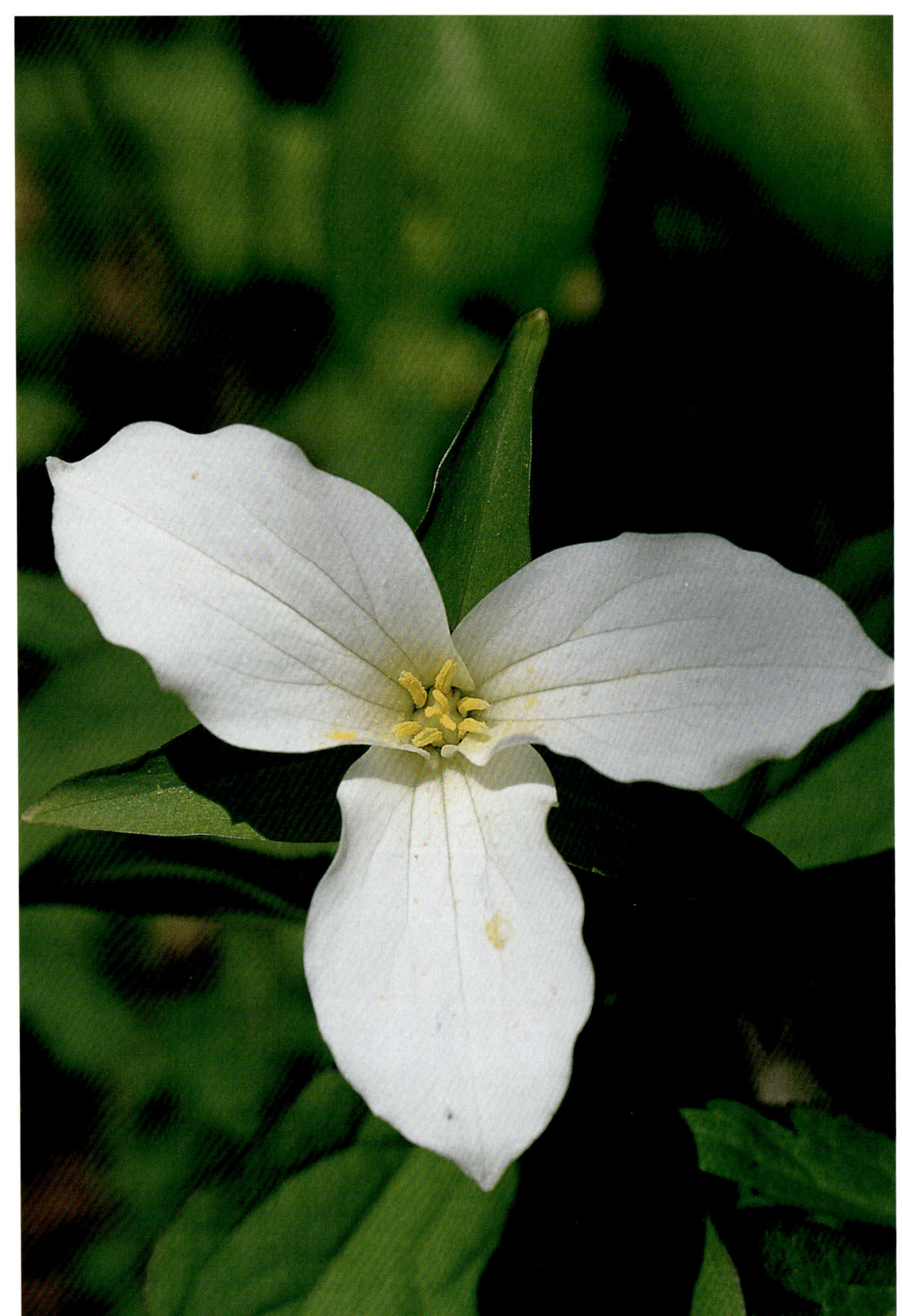

Ontario's official flower, *Trillium grandiflorum,* is named for its large blooms, held upright by foliage. Flowering in April and May, the plant carpets patches of the forest floor throughout the province.

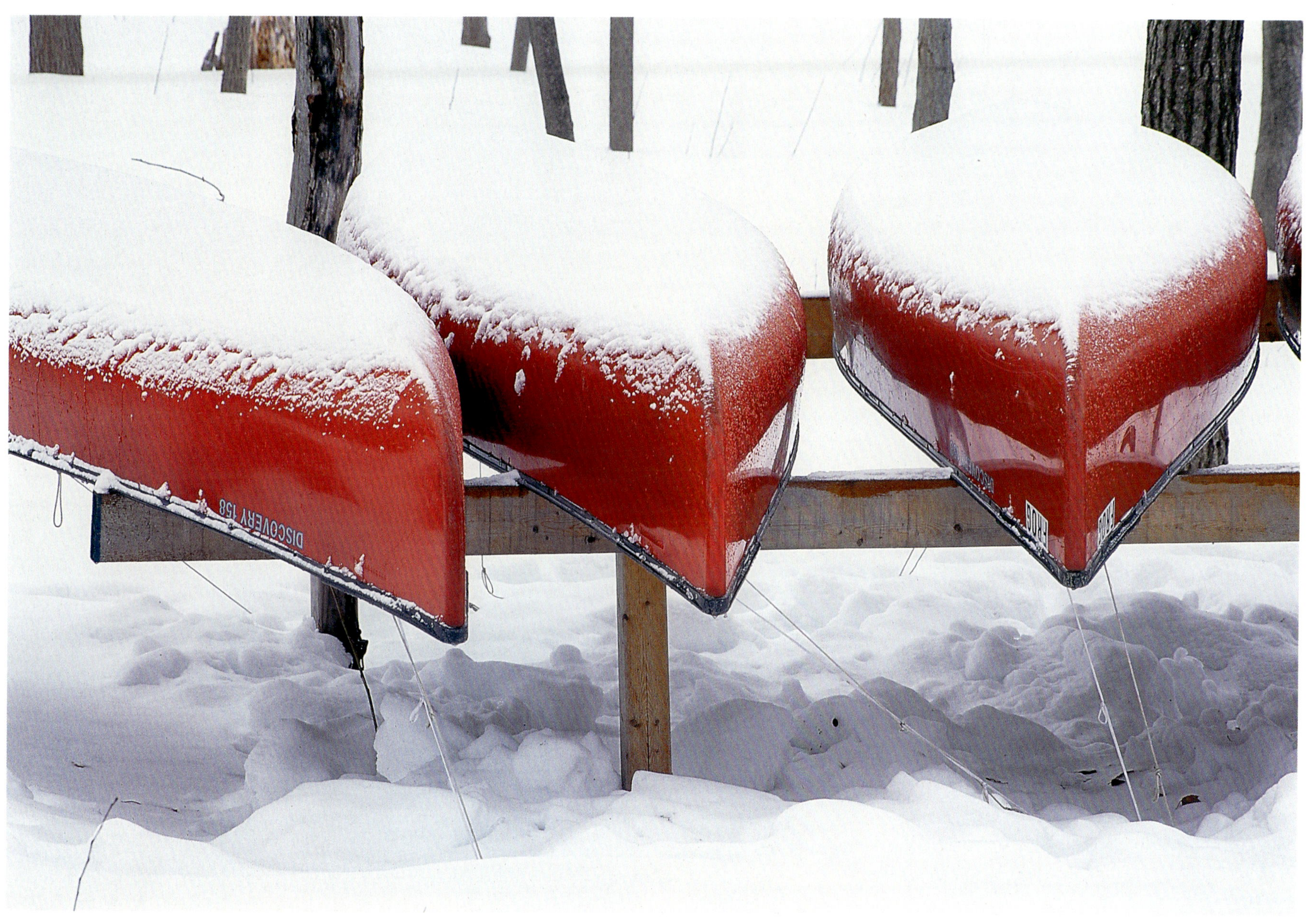

The beach season in Ontario is often short, with the first frost arriving before August is over. In winter, Algonquin Park becomes a destination for snowshoers and cross-country skiers.

History in the Haliburton Highlands is filled with tales of loggers and trappers, hunters and pioneers. Burly lumberjacks once raced logs down the region's rivers, and early settlers hewed clearings from old-growth forests.

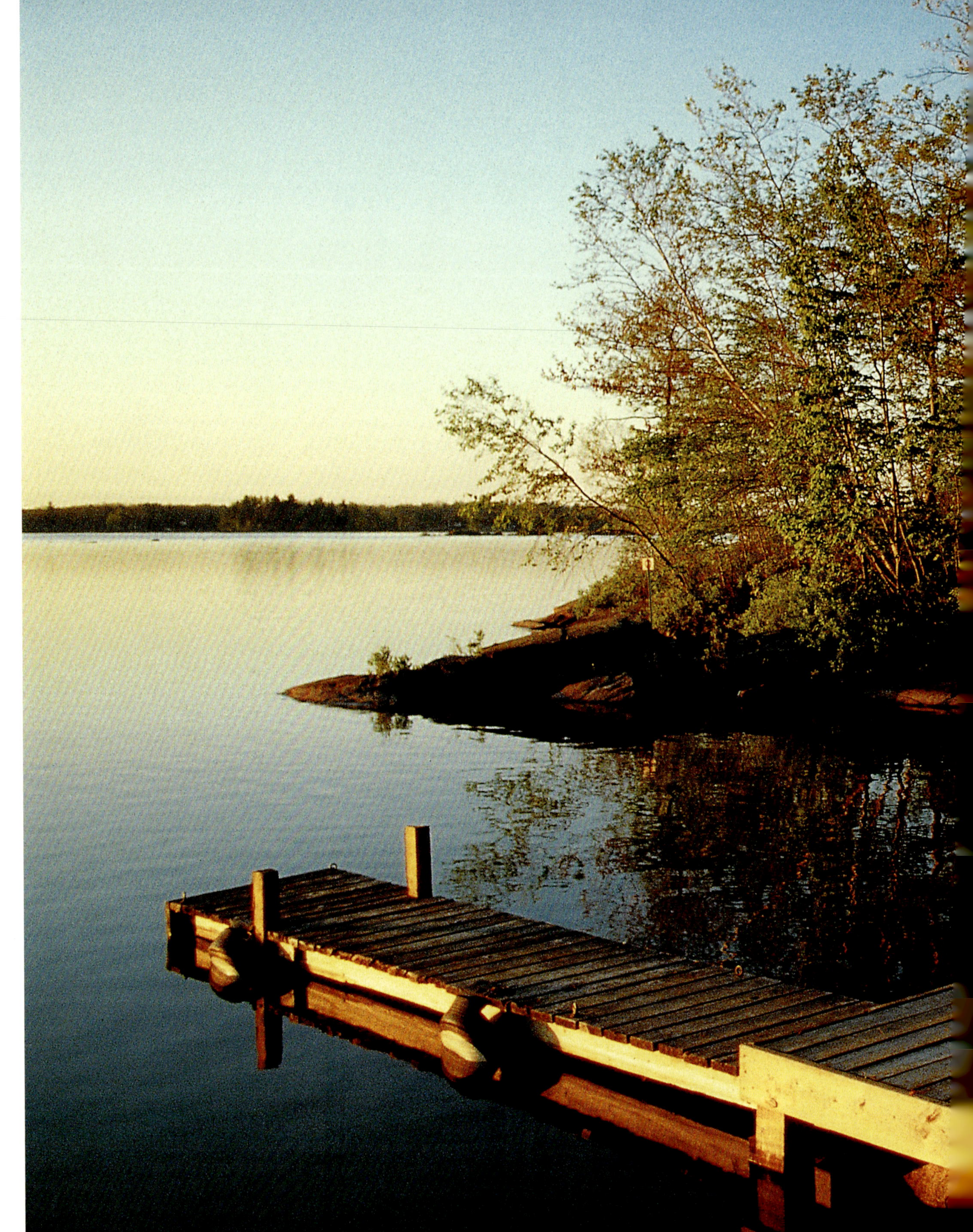

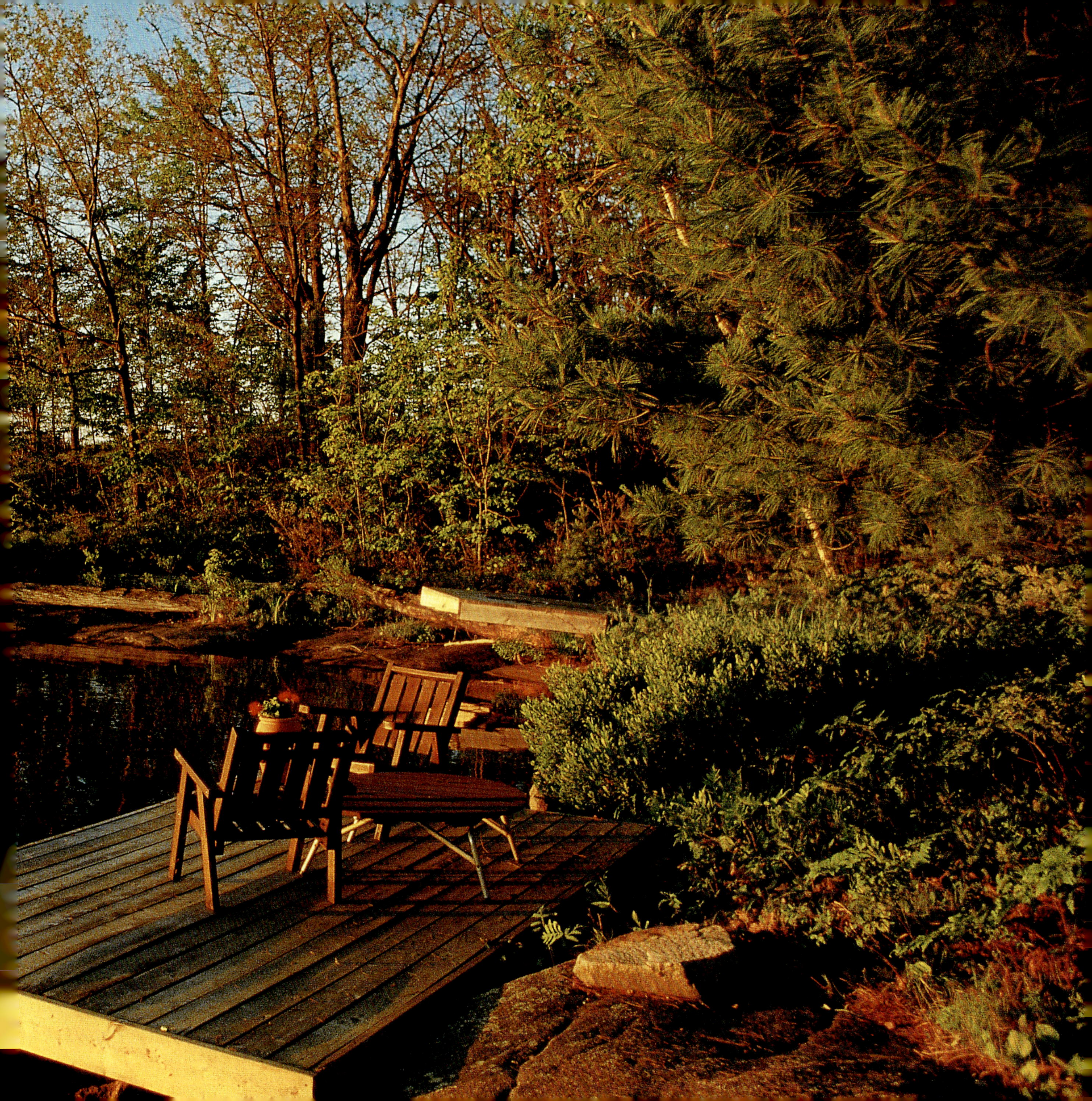

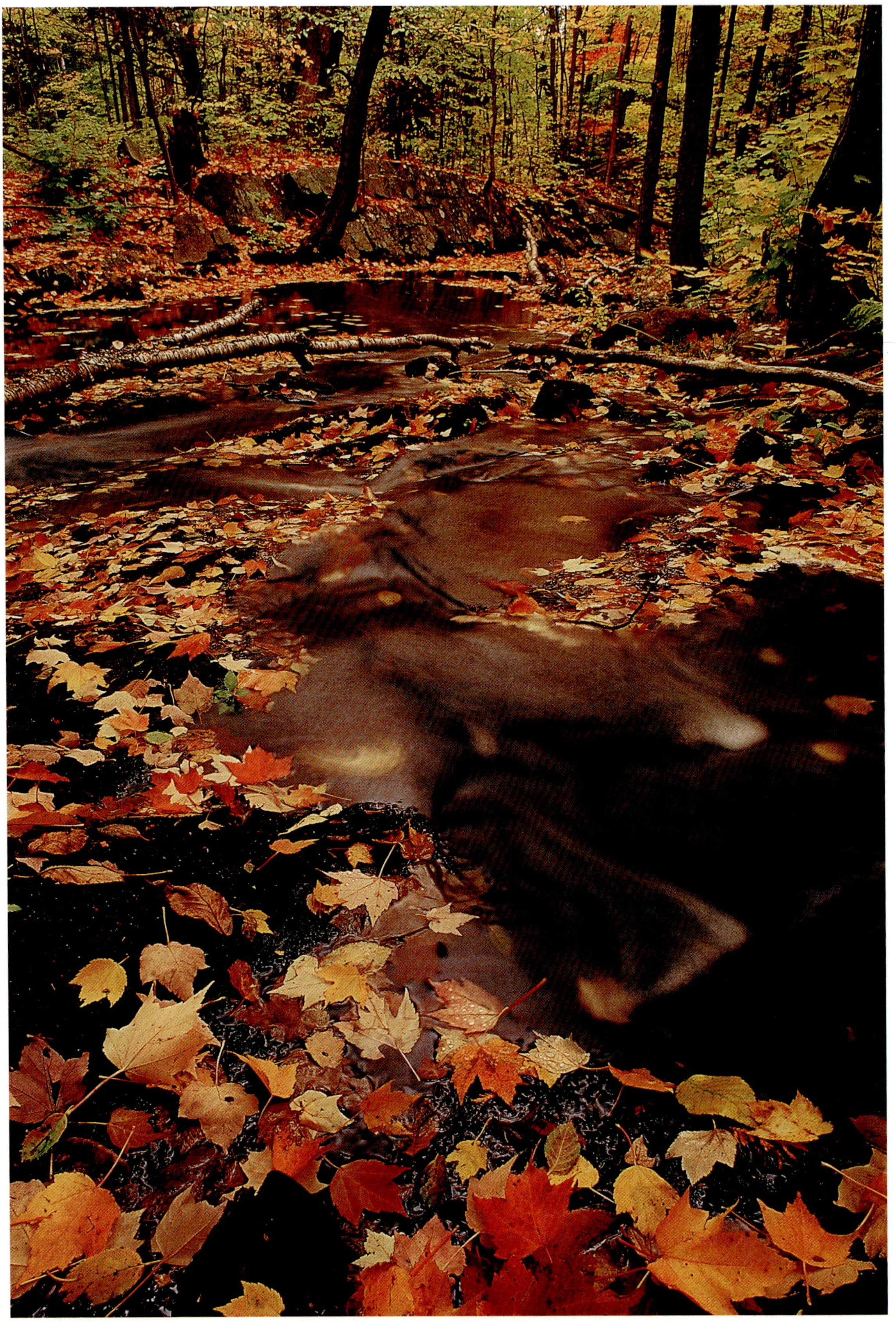

The headwaters of Silent Creek flow from the Haliburton Highlands. The rock beds in this area yield rich finds of gems and minerals, from feldspar to calcite.

FACING PAGE—
A farming and logging town since the 1860s, Haliburton is now a bustling tourist centre, conveniently situated on the route to cottage country.

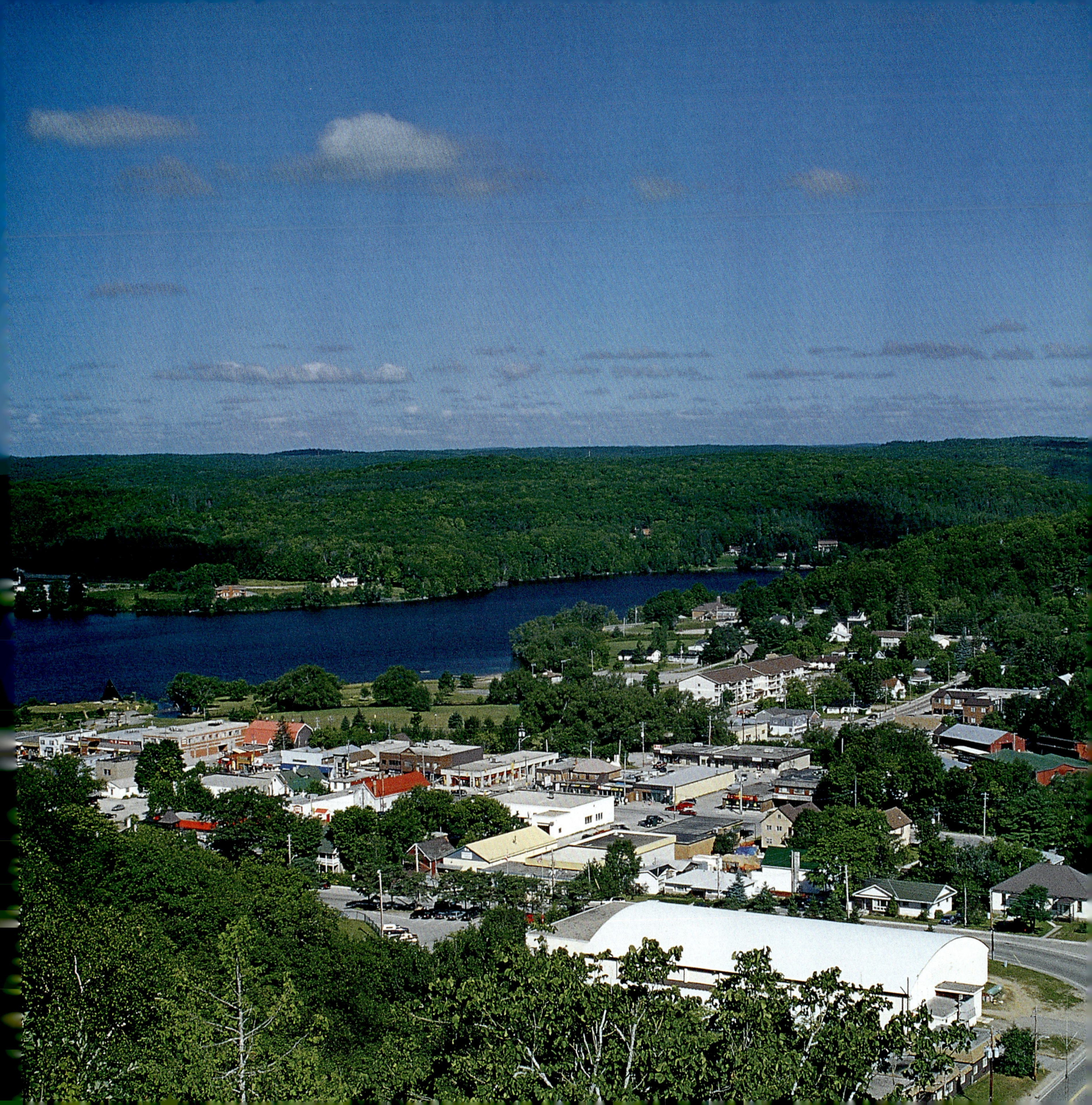

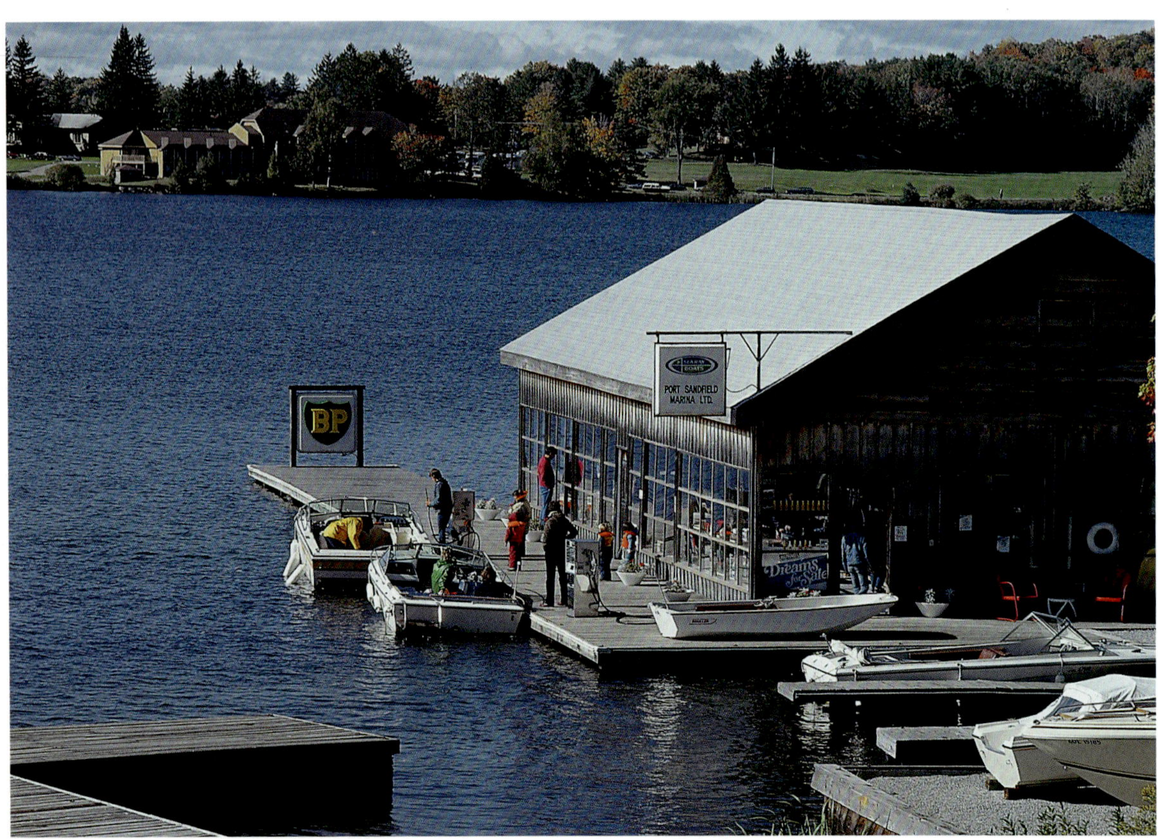

The wooden boat building industry began in the Muskoka Lakes region soon after settlers arrived. At the Port Sandfield Marina, the tradition continues—new wooden canoes and heritage-style boats are still being launched.

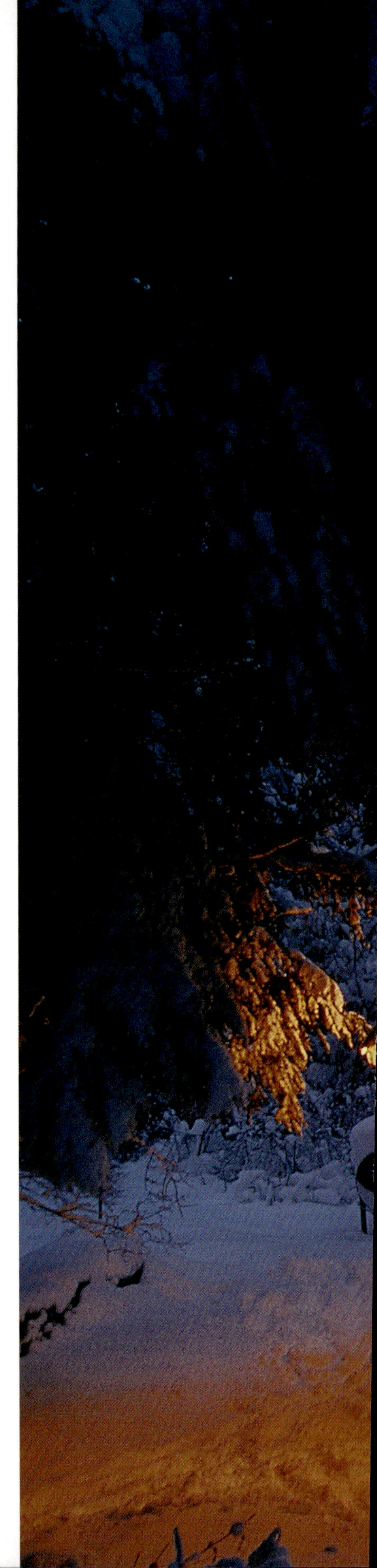

Winter snow blankets a cabin on the shores of Lake Joseph. French fur traders explored this land centuries ago, as they paddled their way along the connected channels of lakes Joseph, Rosseau, and Muskoka.

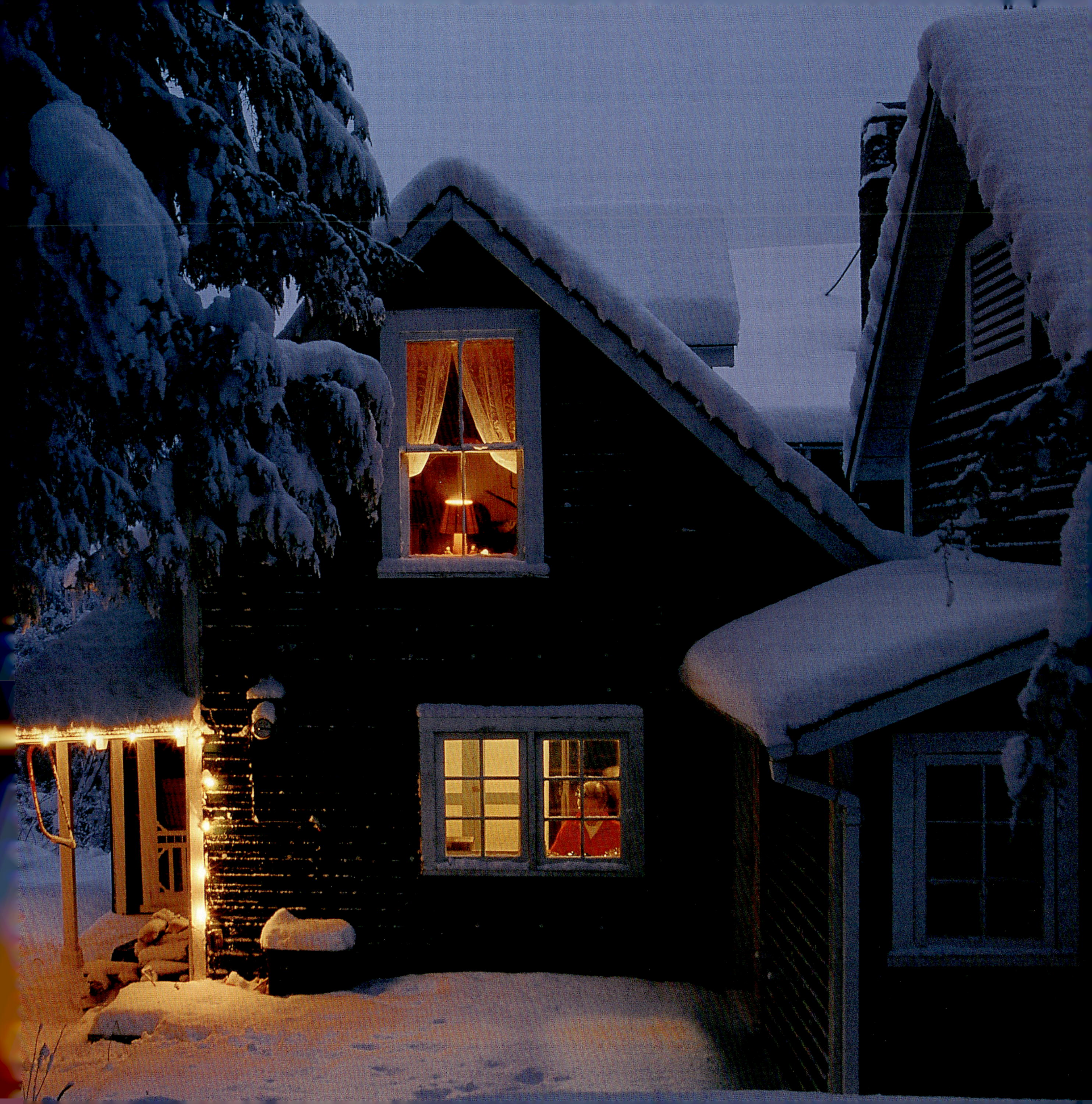

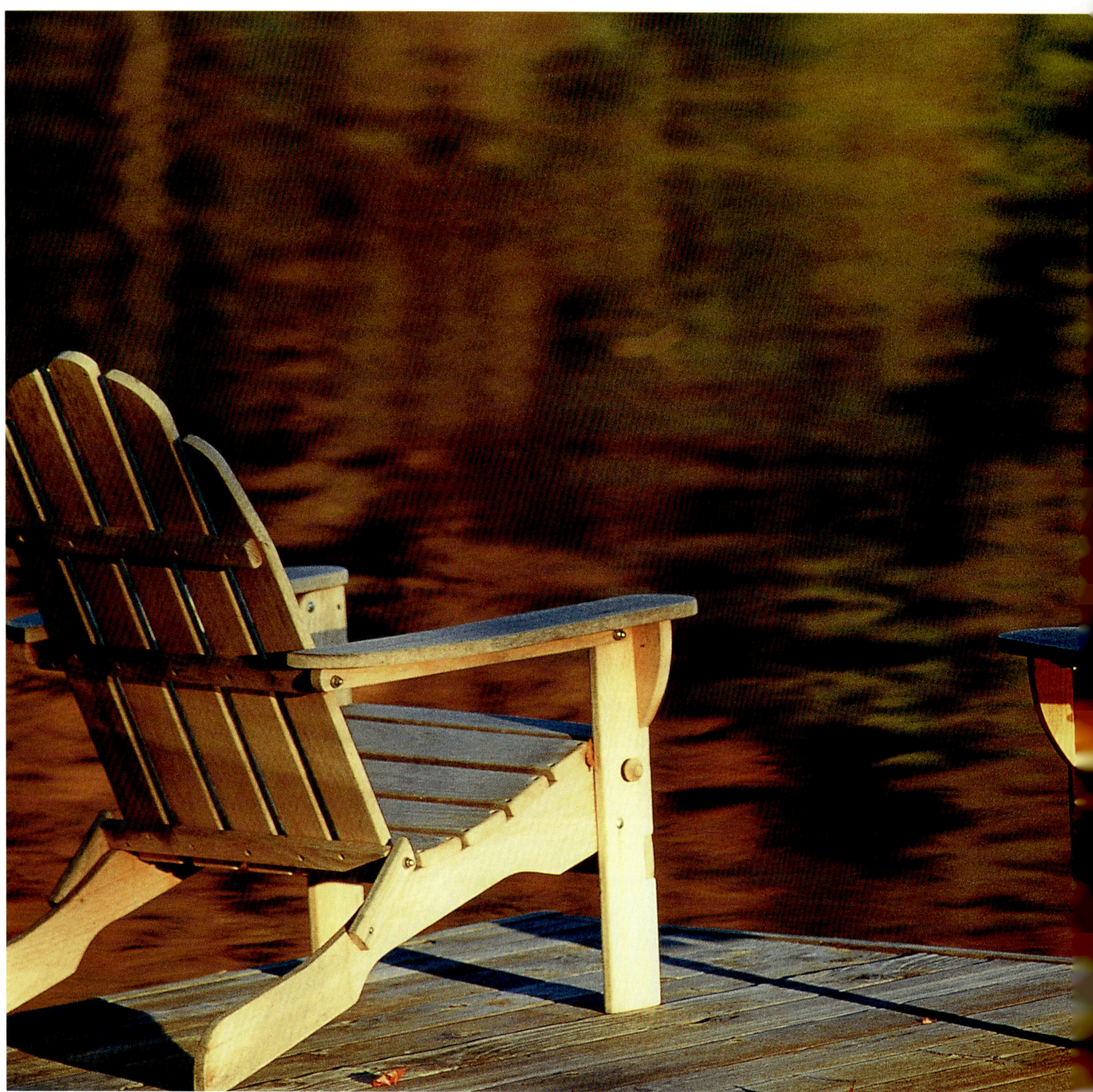

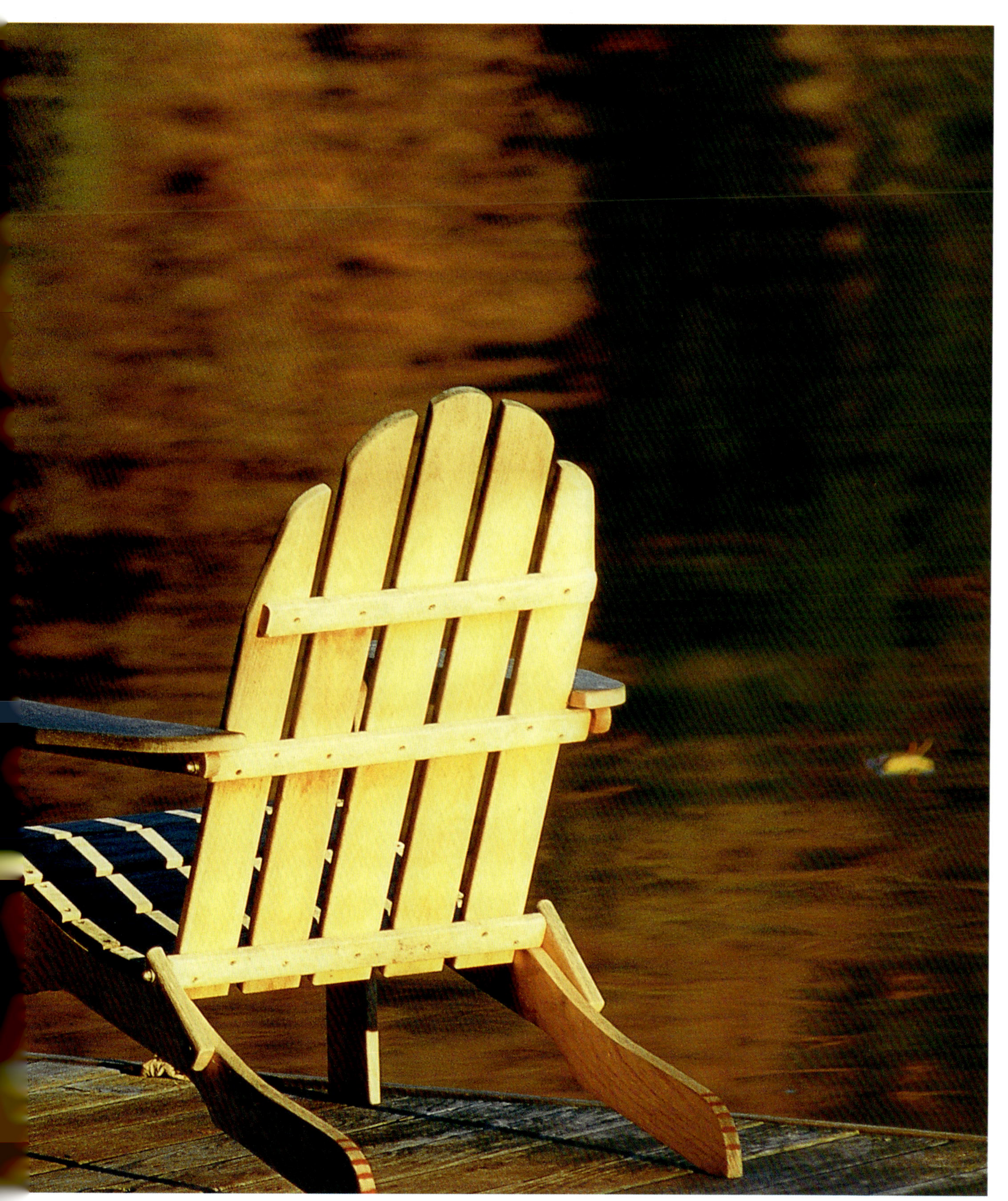

Muskoka chairs (or Adirondack chairs, depending on which side of the border you're sitting) are an Ontario cottage essential. According to local legend, they were invented in 1900 by American Thomas Lee, who created several prototypes for his family to choose from.

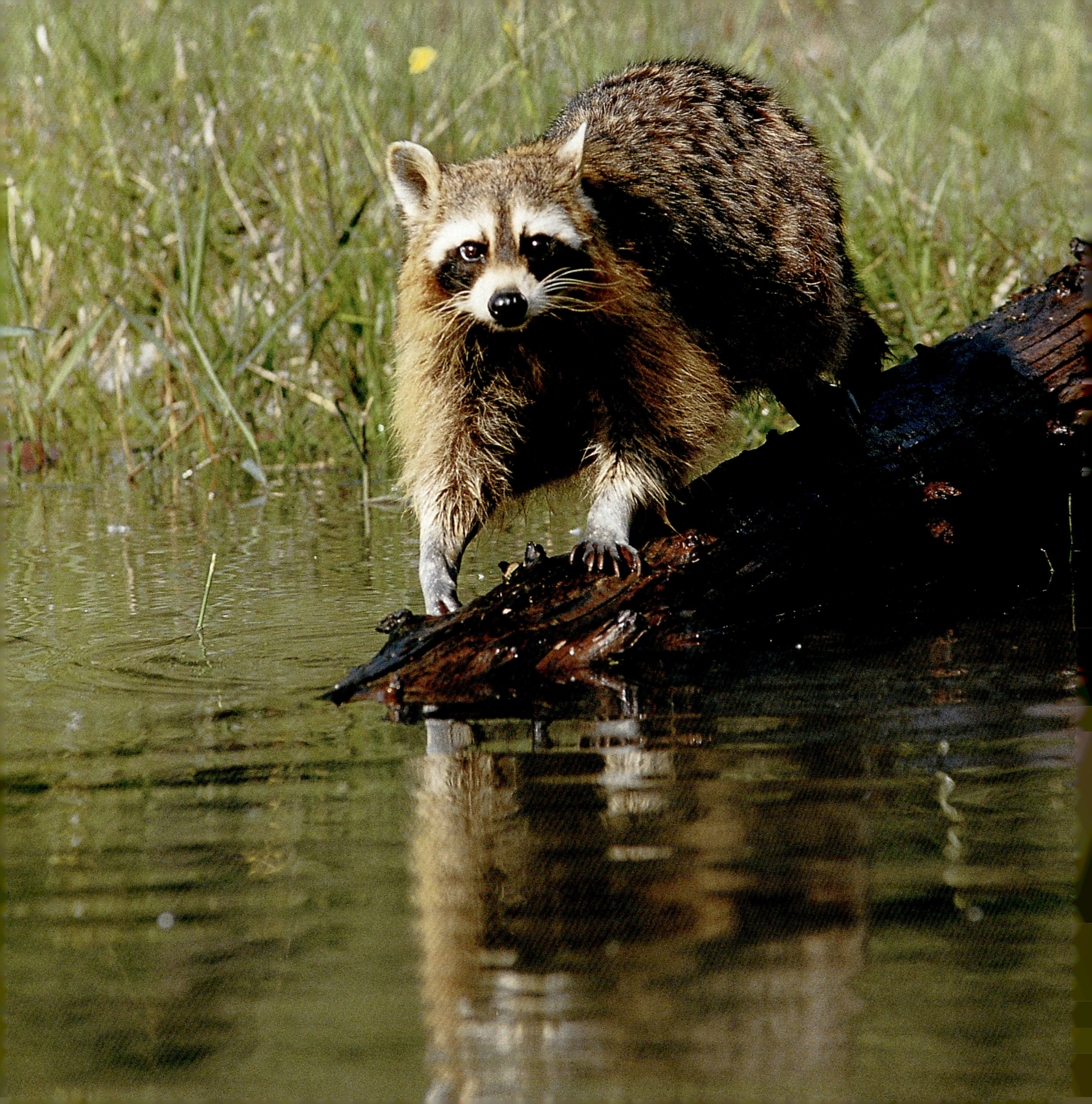

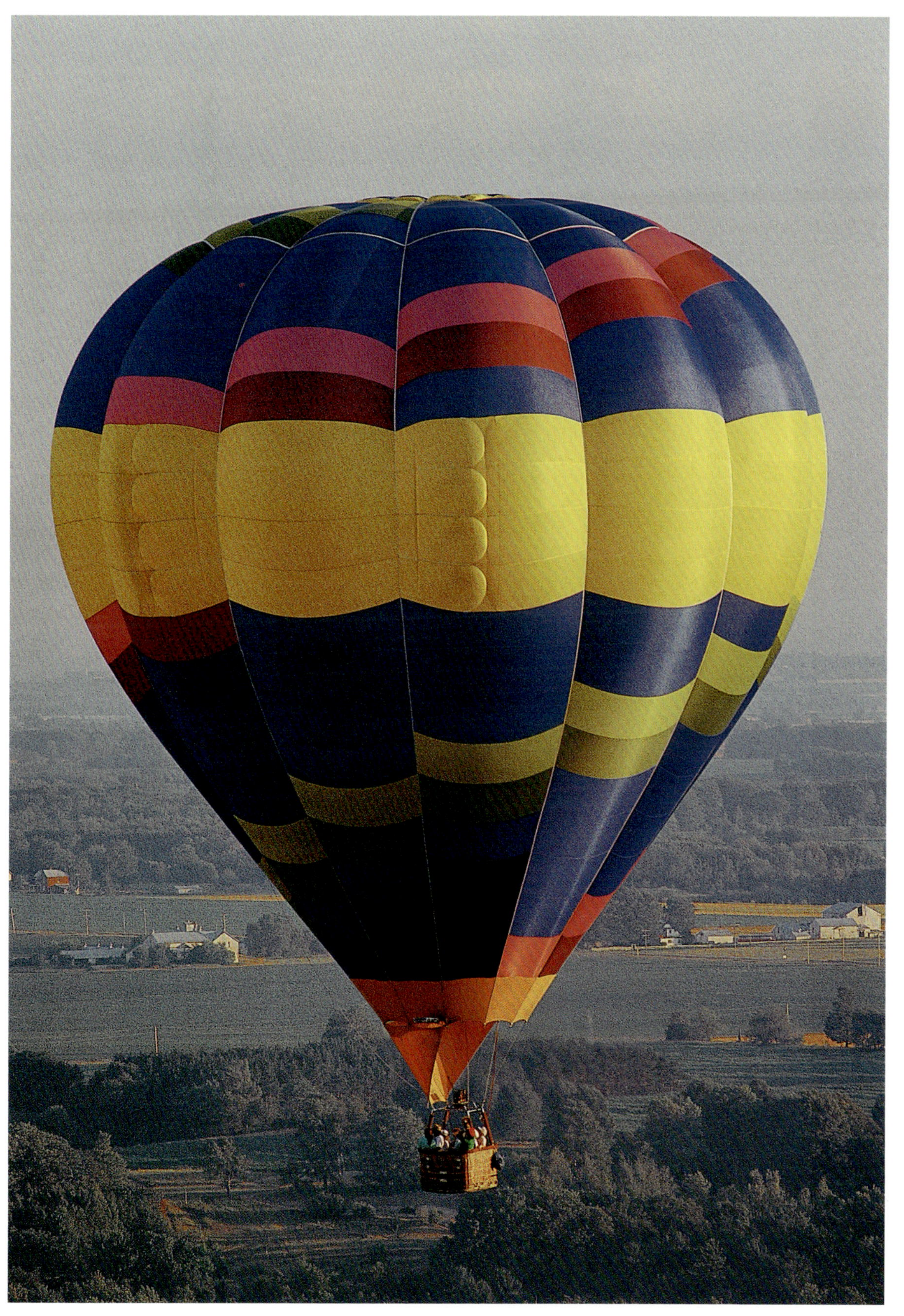

A hot-air balloon ride offers a panoramic view of the province's forests. More than 100 of the parks that protect Ontario's woods and shorelines are open to the public.

Facing Page— The raccoon was named by the Algonquian people who once fished and hunted Ontario's forests. Their word *arakun* translates as "scratches with his hand," a reference to the way raccoons use their paws to crack and "wash" their food.

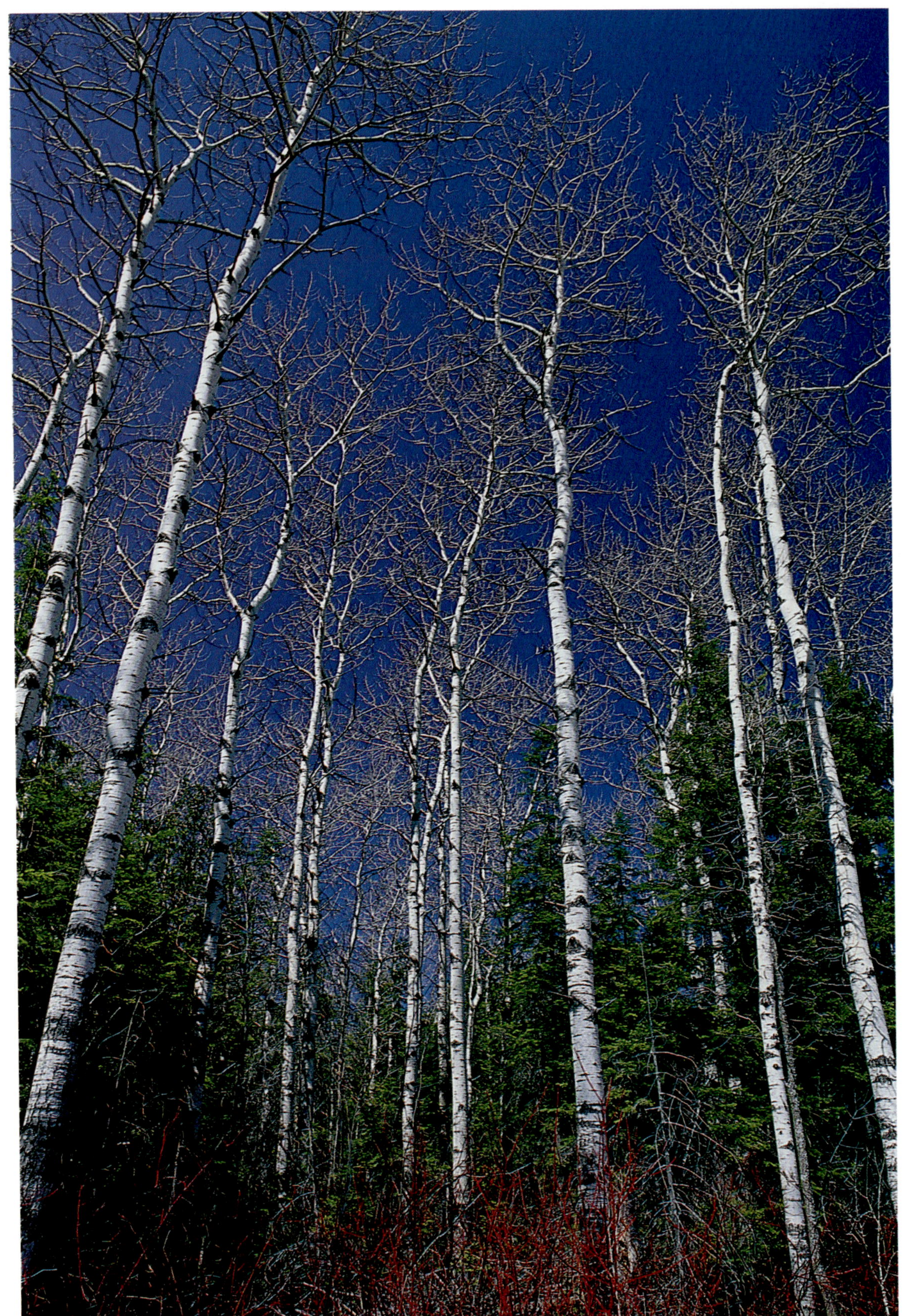

Four hundred million years ago, the land that is now Bruce Peninsula National Park was the floor of a shallow sea, criss-crossed with coral reefs and home to thousands of plants and crustaceans. The fossils remain embedded in the cliffs today.

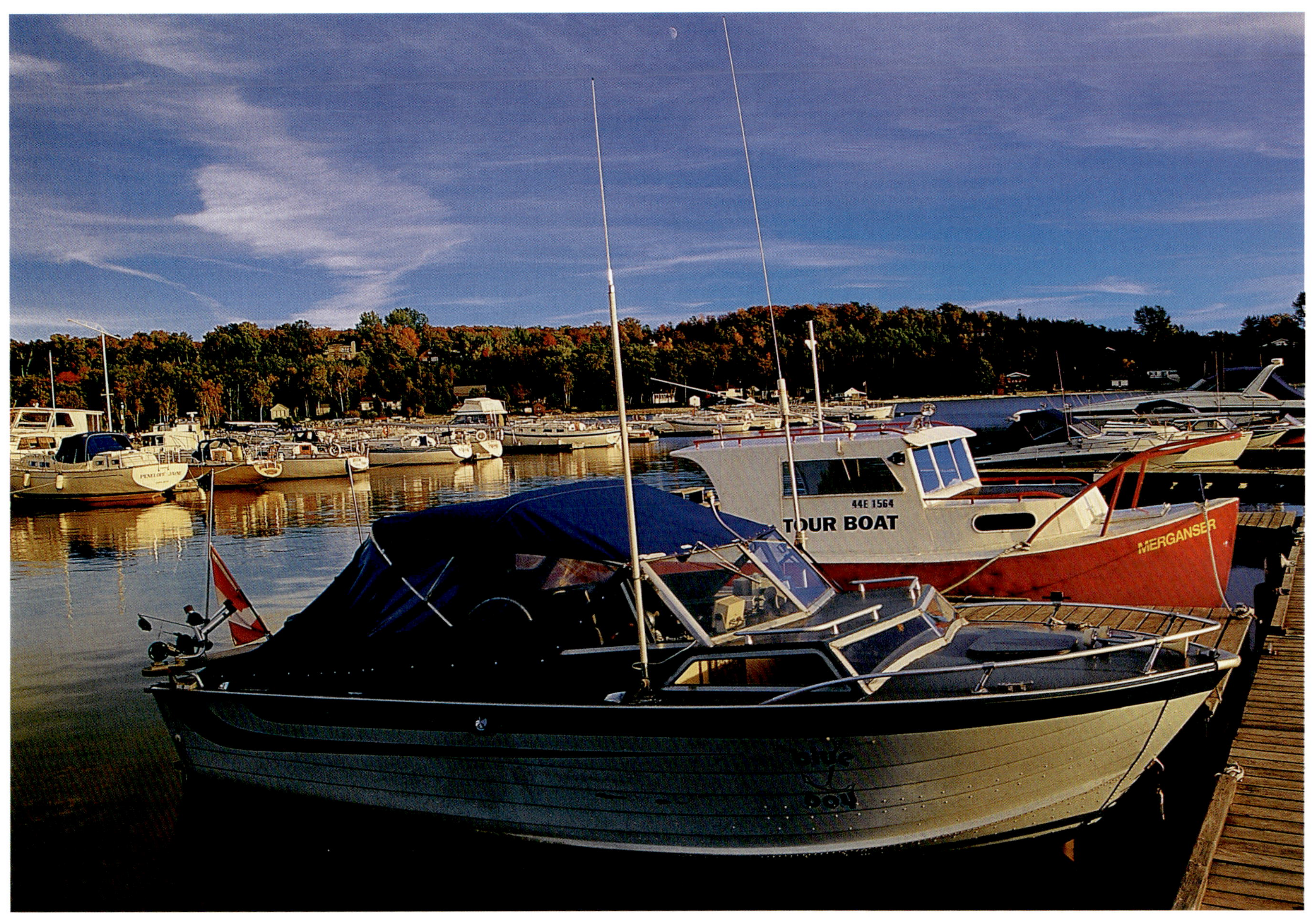

Sheltered below the cliffs of the Niagara Escarpment, Lion's Head lies along the Bruce Trail. Once a stop for the passenger vessels and shipping lines that plied the Great Lakes in the nineteenth and early twentieth centuries, the port is now packed with pleasure vessels.

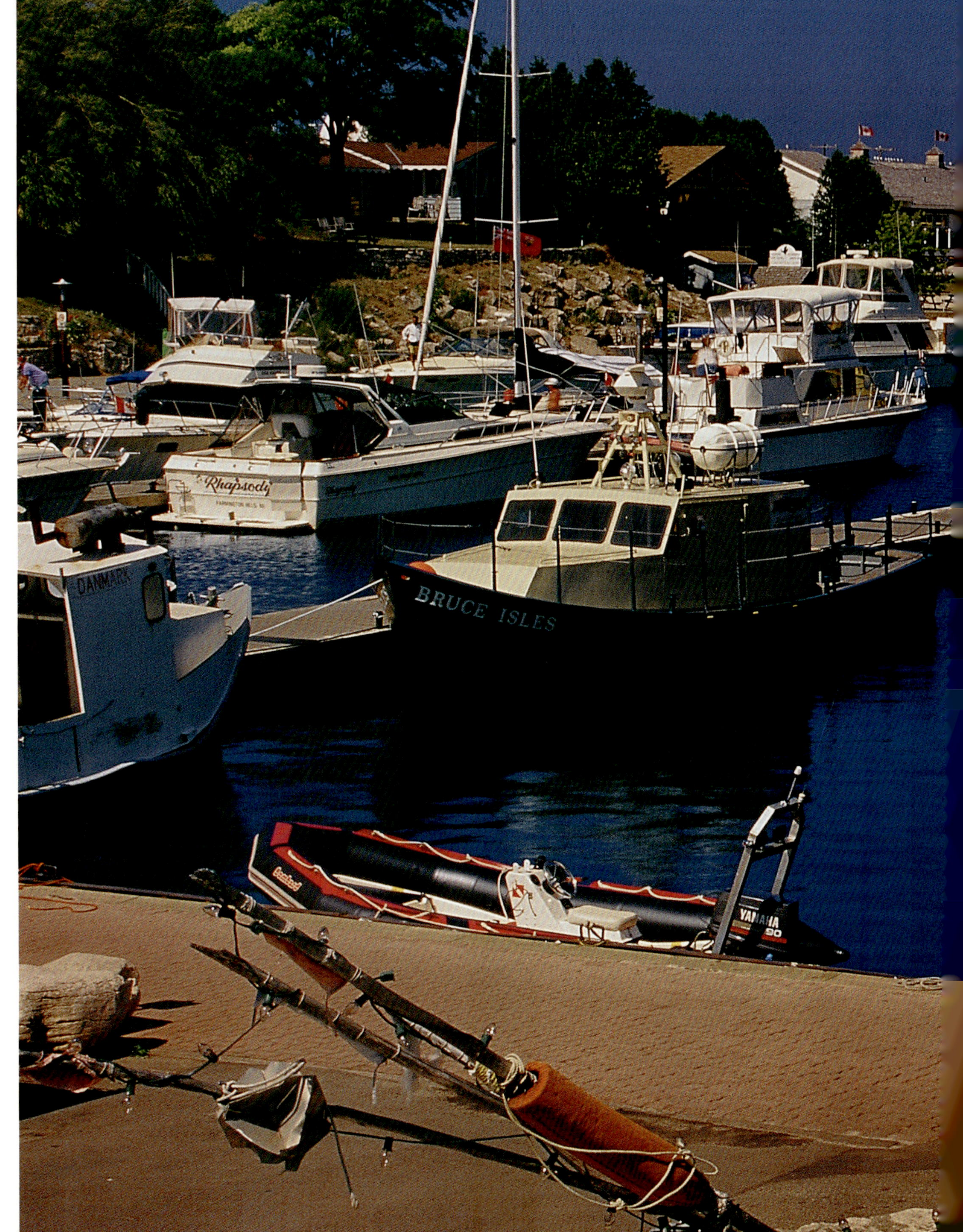

From one side of Little Tub Harbour, hikers embark on the 749-kilometre (465-mile) Bruce Trail through Bruce Peninsula National Park. The trail traces the stony spine of the Niagara Escarpment south to Queenston Heights.

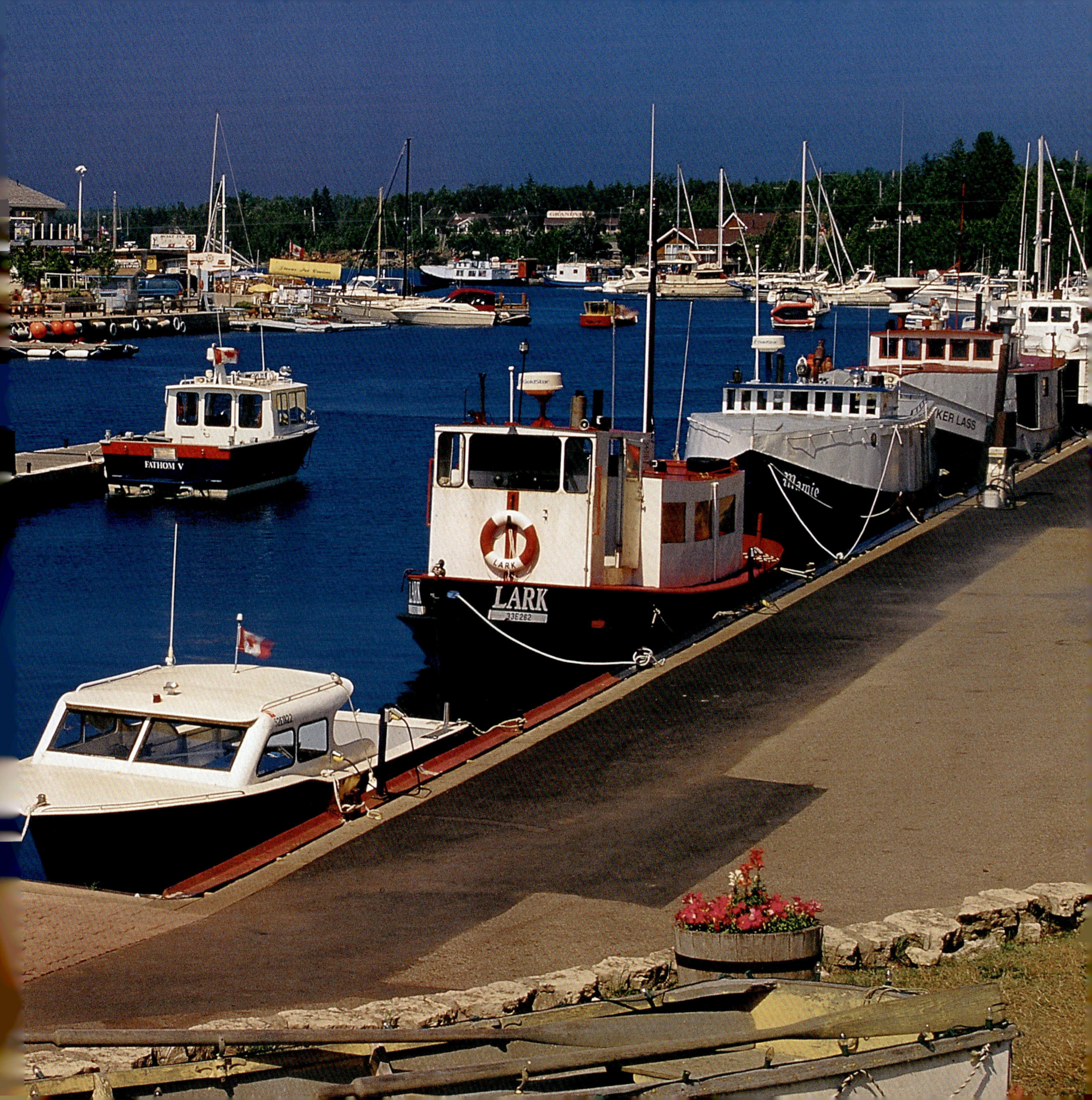
FATHOM V
LARK
33E262
Mamie

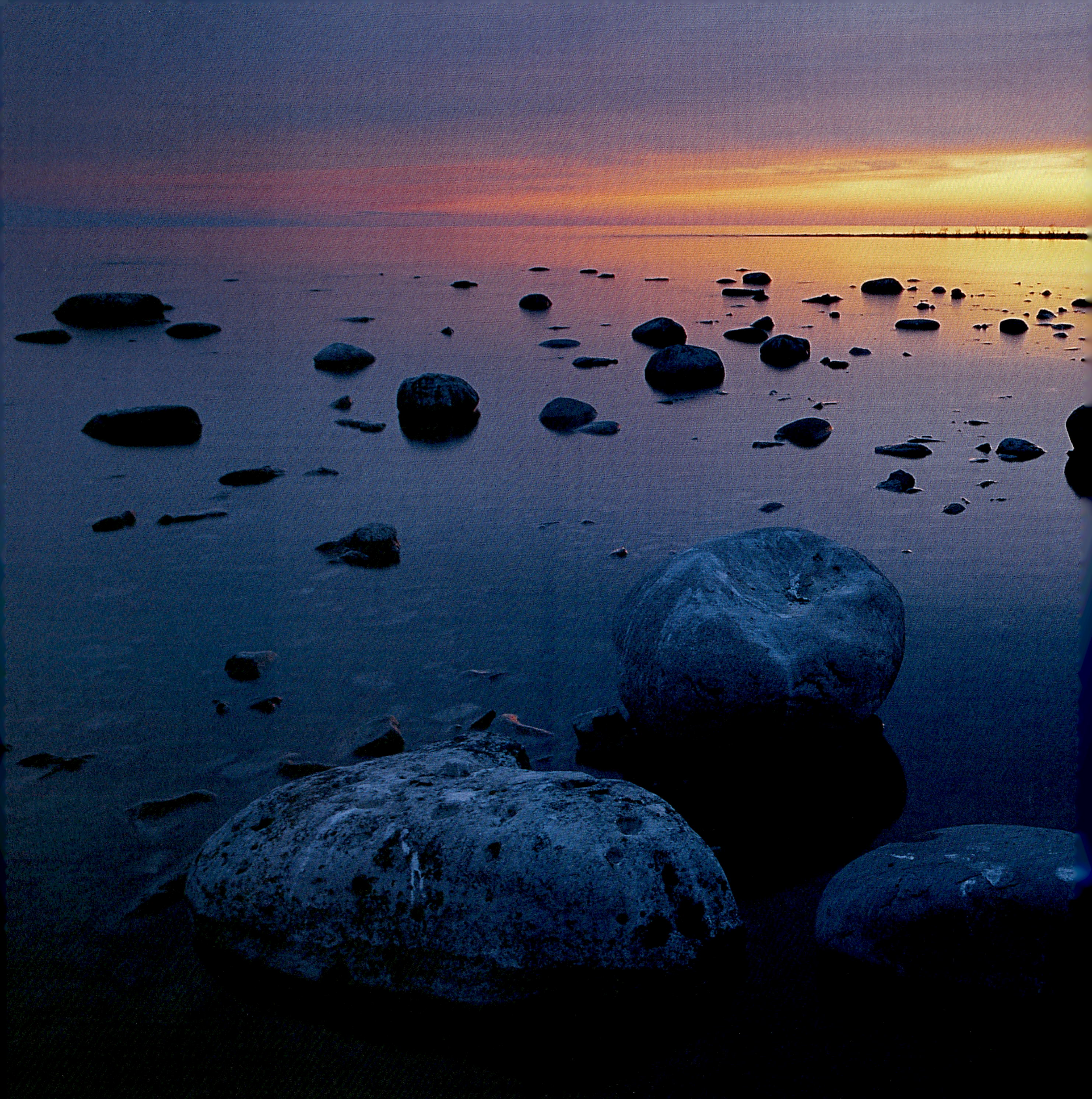

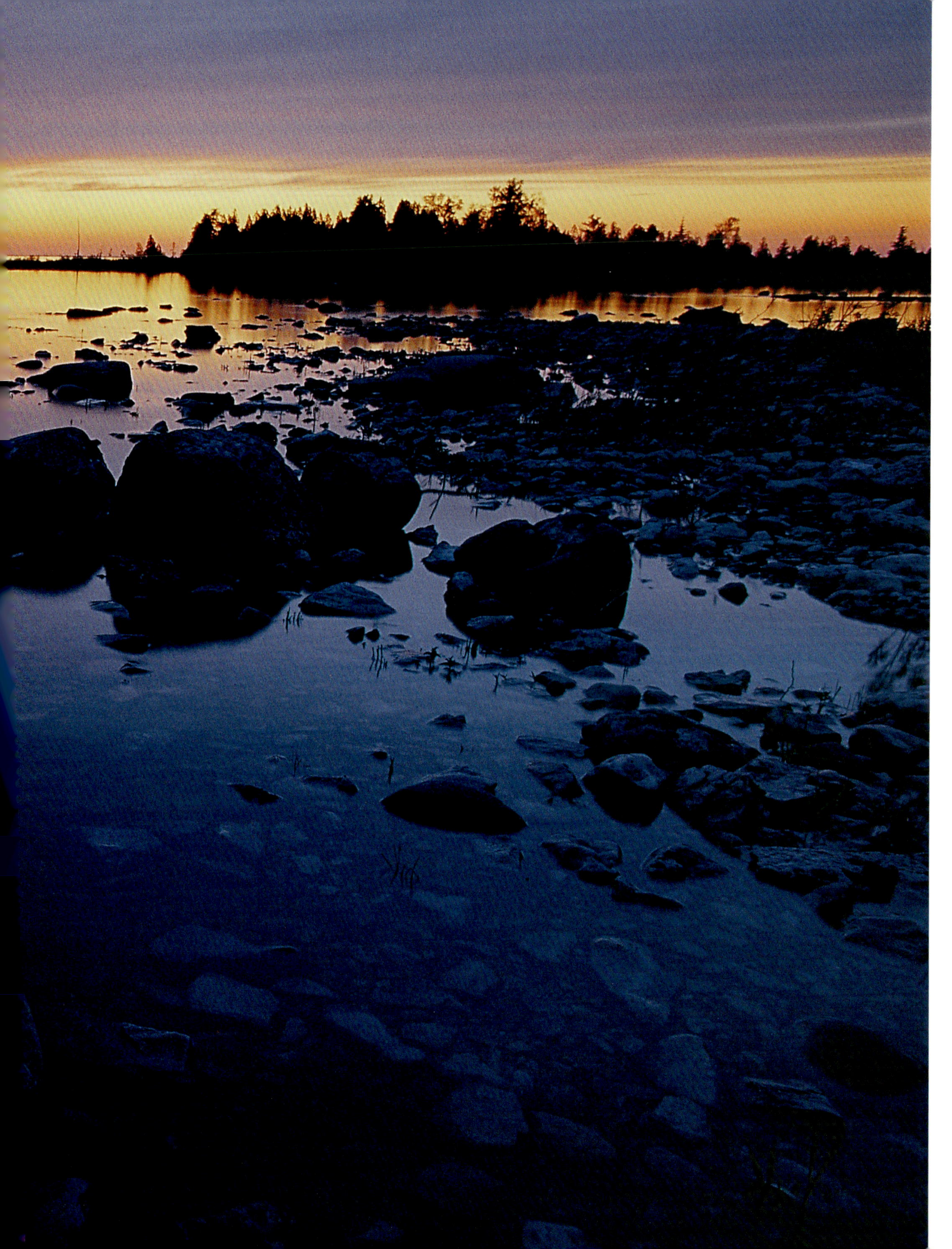

The treacherous waters of Lake Huron near Tobermory conceal the remains of more than 21 vessels that met their end here in the early days of shipping on the Great Lakes. The wrecks make this one of Ontario's most popular diving locations.

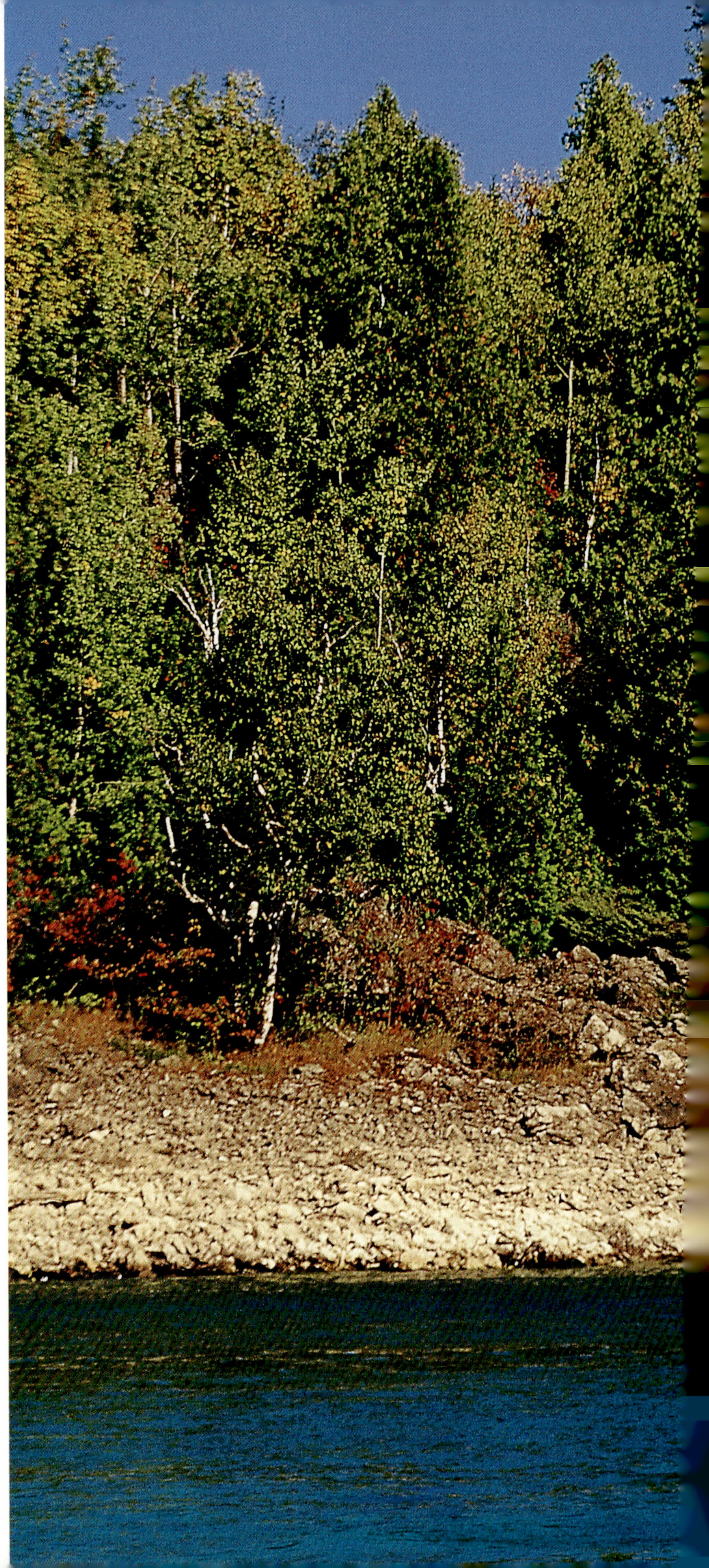

Kayakers explore the shore of Lake Huron, just one possible trip among hundreds throughout the province. Algonquin Park alone boasts more than 1,500 kilometres (930 miles) of paddling routes.

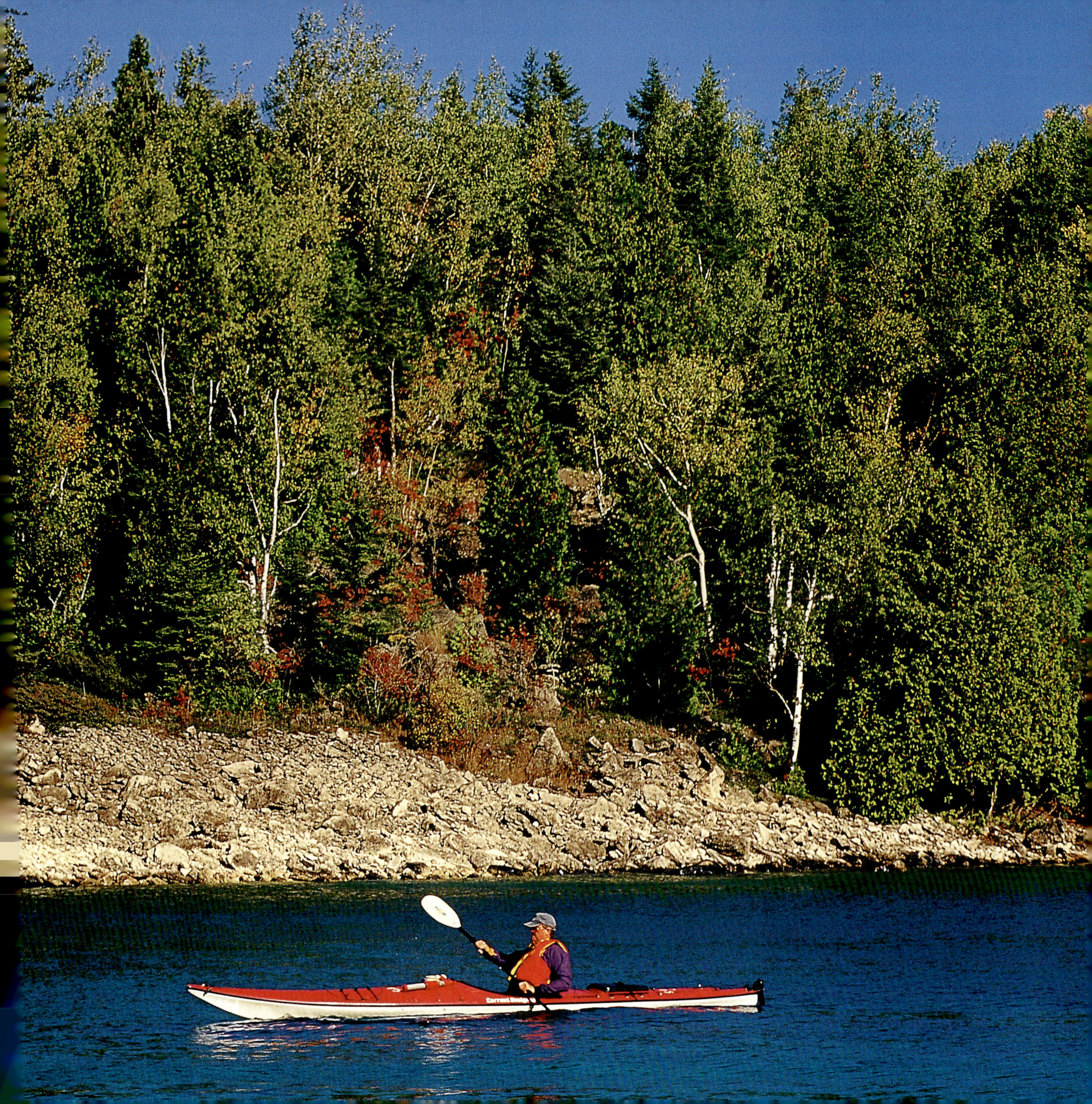

St. Catharines was first settled by Loyalists John Hainer and Jacob Dittrick in 1790 and it grew steadily as a farming and commercial centre. It retains its agricultural roots, although, with a population of more than 130,000 people, the city is now the largest in the Niagara region.

Facing Page—
Known as Ontario's Garden City, St. Catharines has a bird sanctuary, botanical gardens, a rose garden with more than 1,300 plants, and the popular Lakeside Park, where families and visitors retreat for picnics and strolls along the beach.

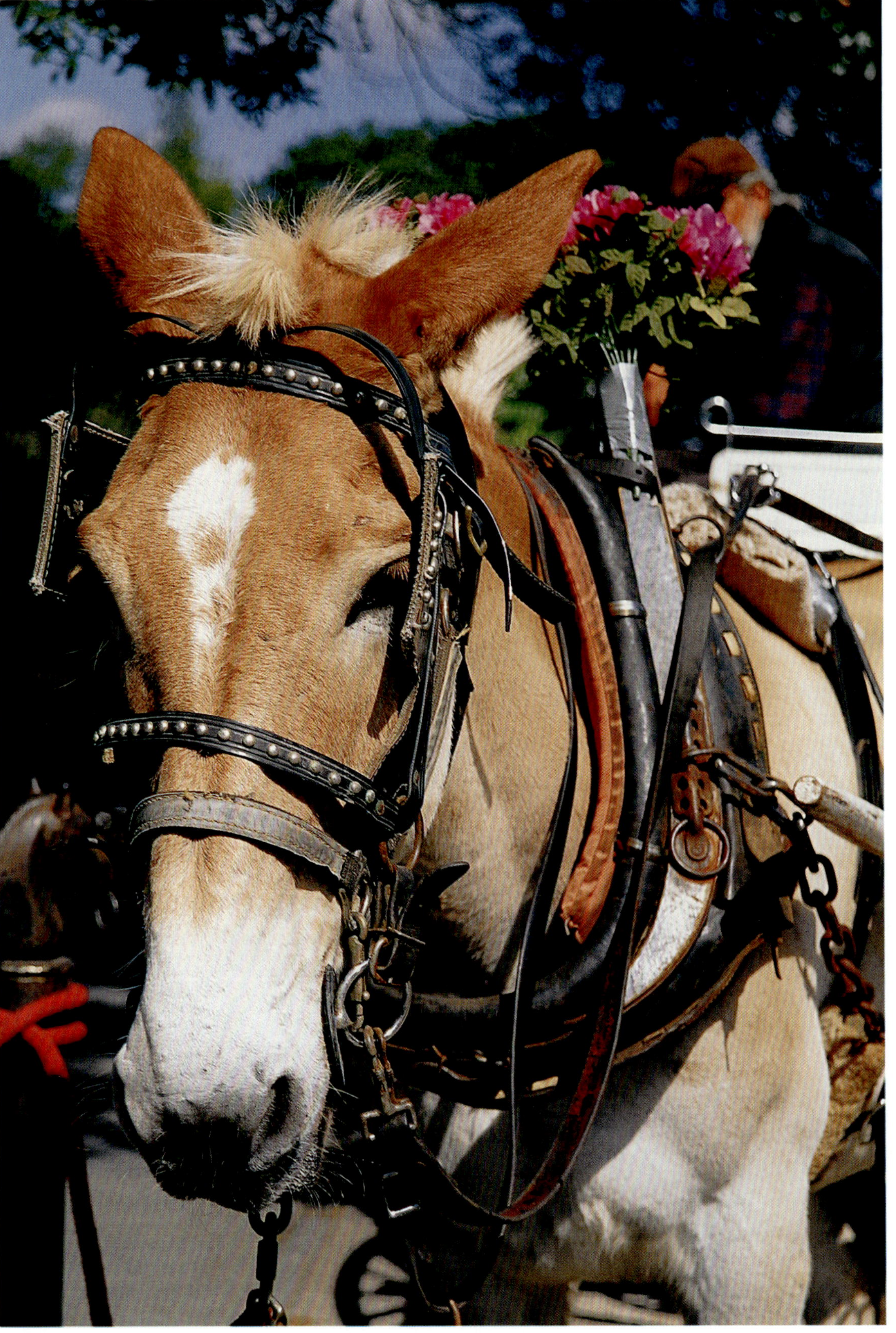

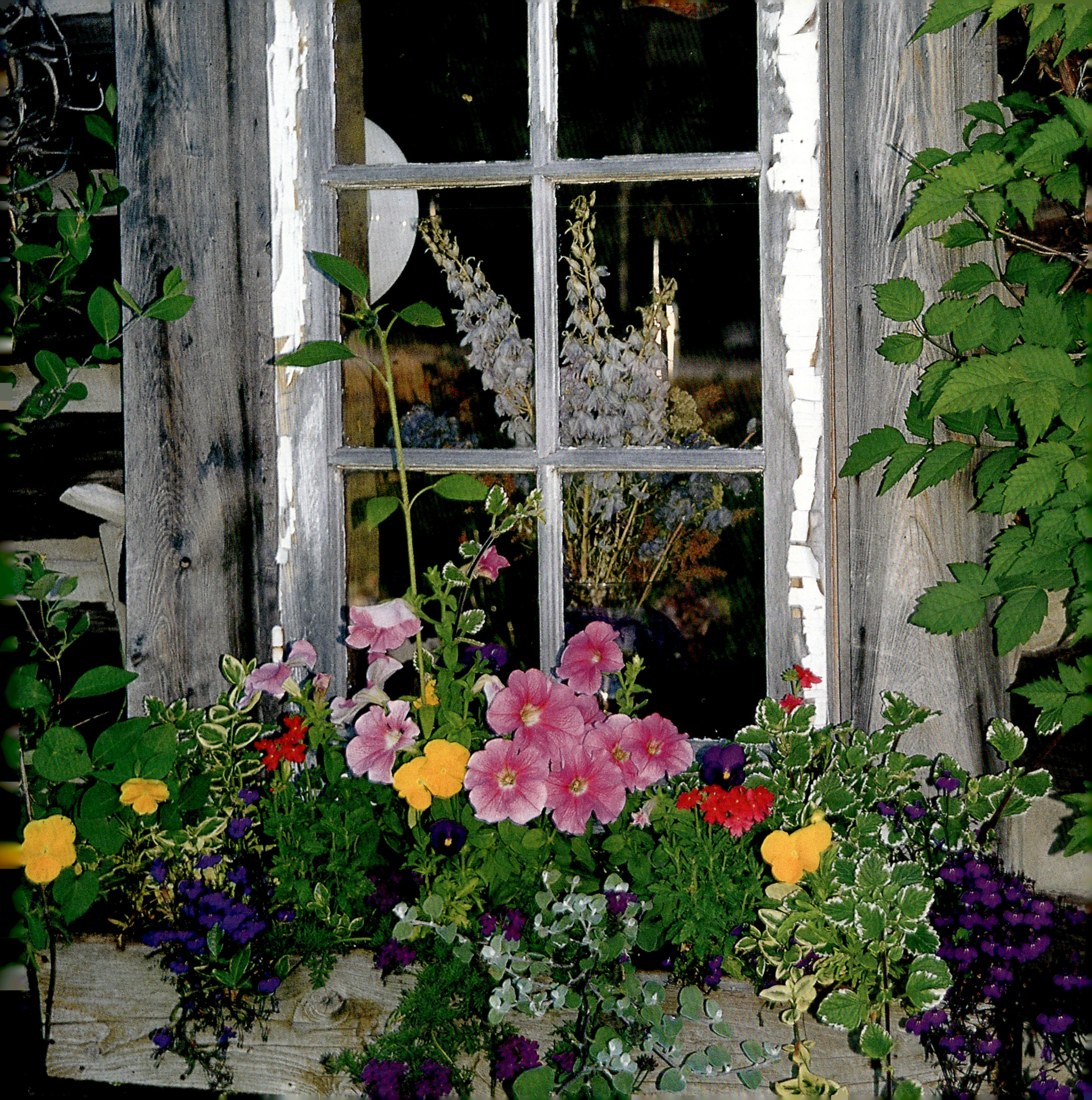

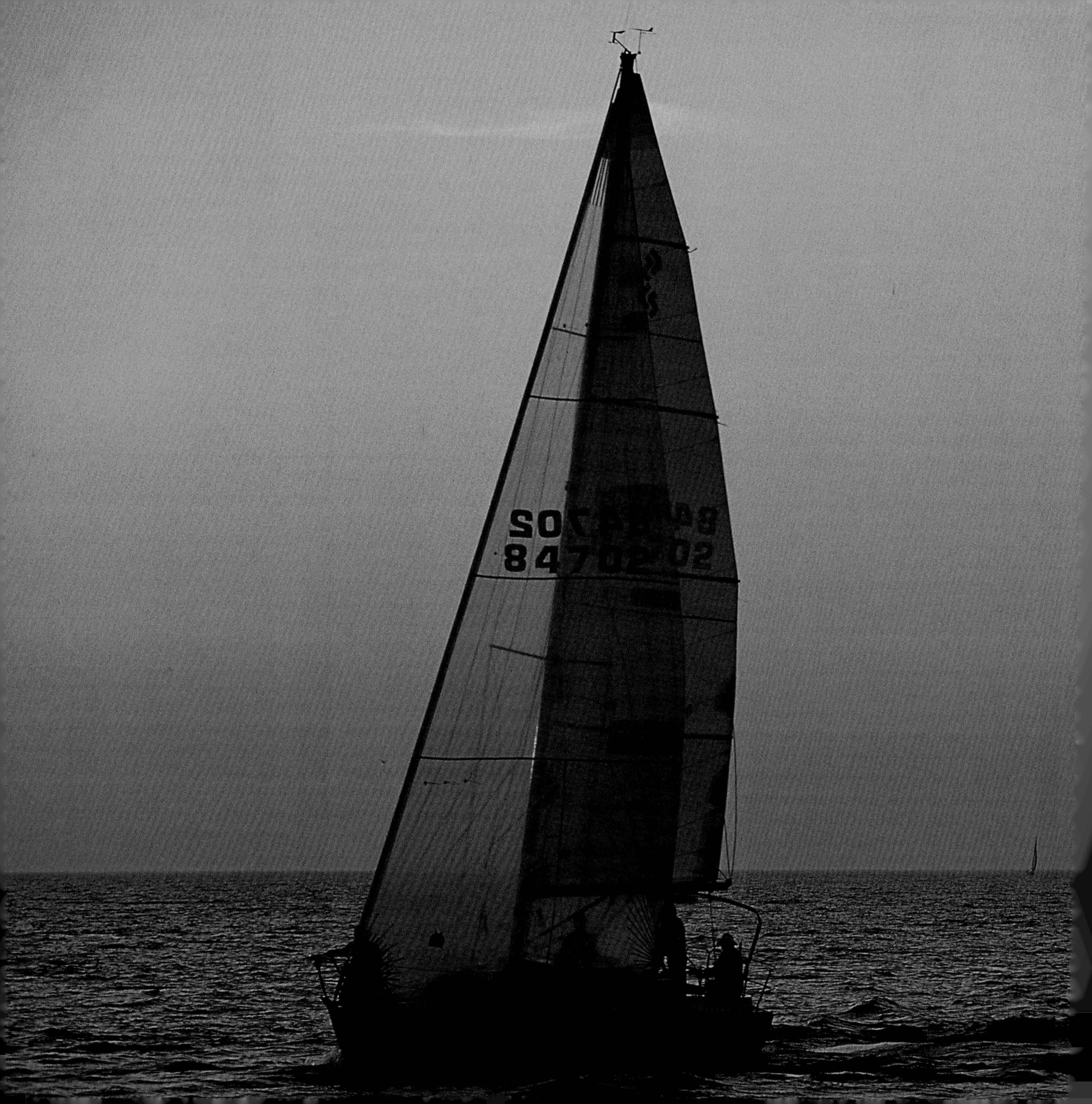
84702

Fishing and sailing enthusiasts take to the waters of Lake Ontario from the St. Catharines Marina. Almost 200 floating docks at the marina cater both to privately owned vessels and charter tour boats.

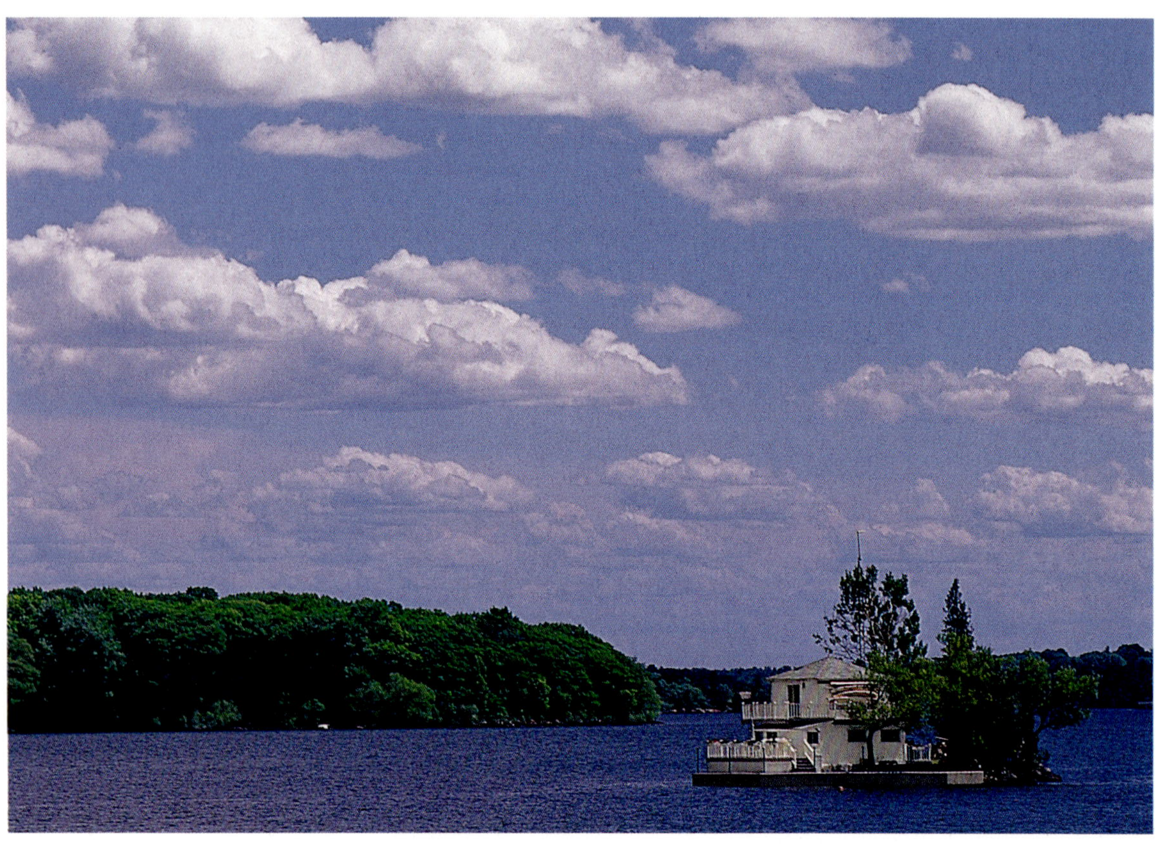

The Thousand Islands are actually 1,800 islands, some only large enough for a few trees or a single cottage clinging to the shore.

American business tycoon George C. Boldt commissioned Boldt Castle in the Thousand Islands for his wife, Louise. It was to have swimming pools, verandahs, underground passages, and other luxuries. When Louise died suddenly in 1904, the heartbroken man left the castle unfinished.

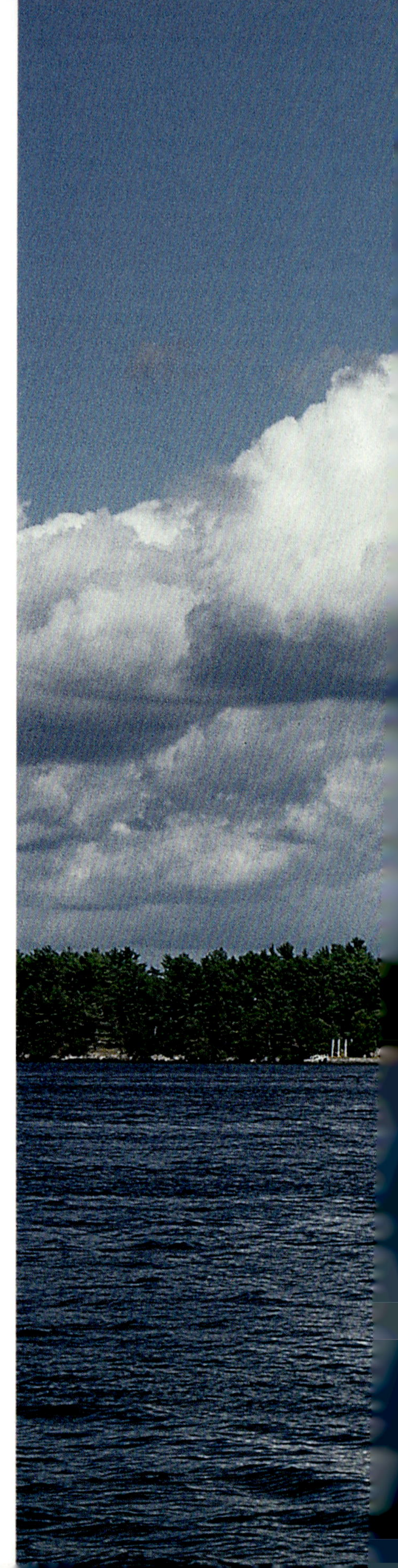

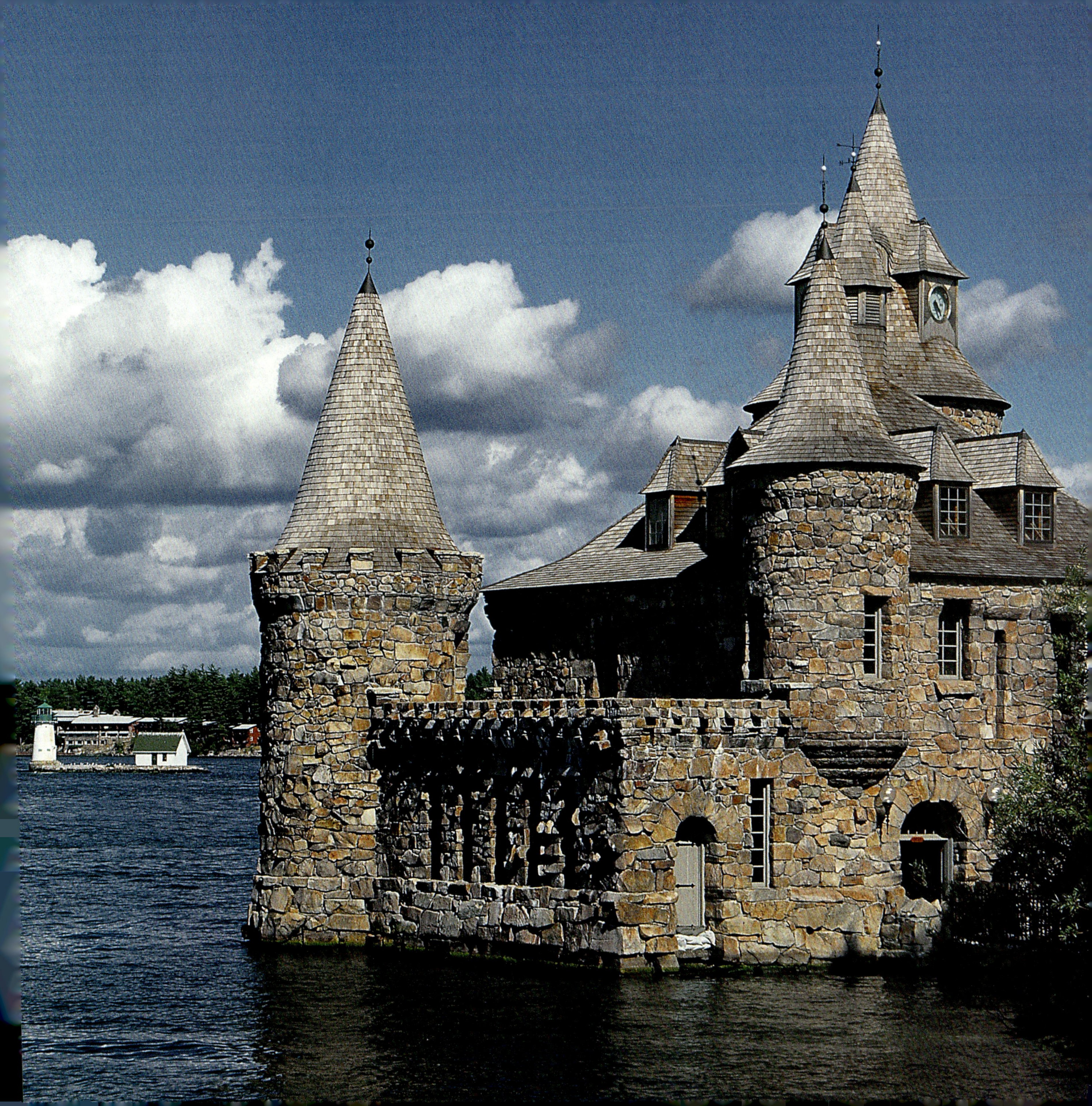

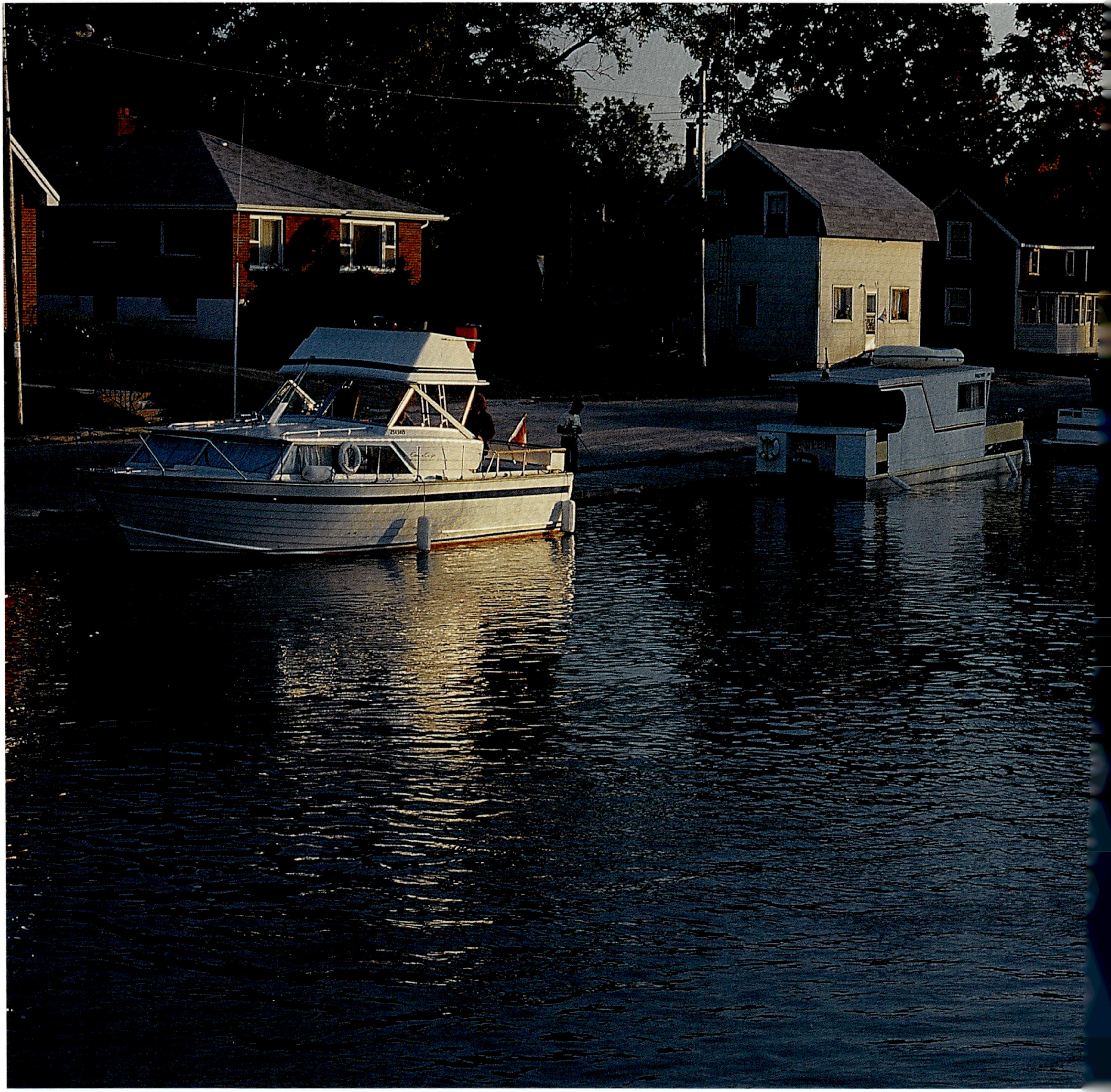

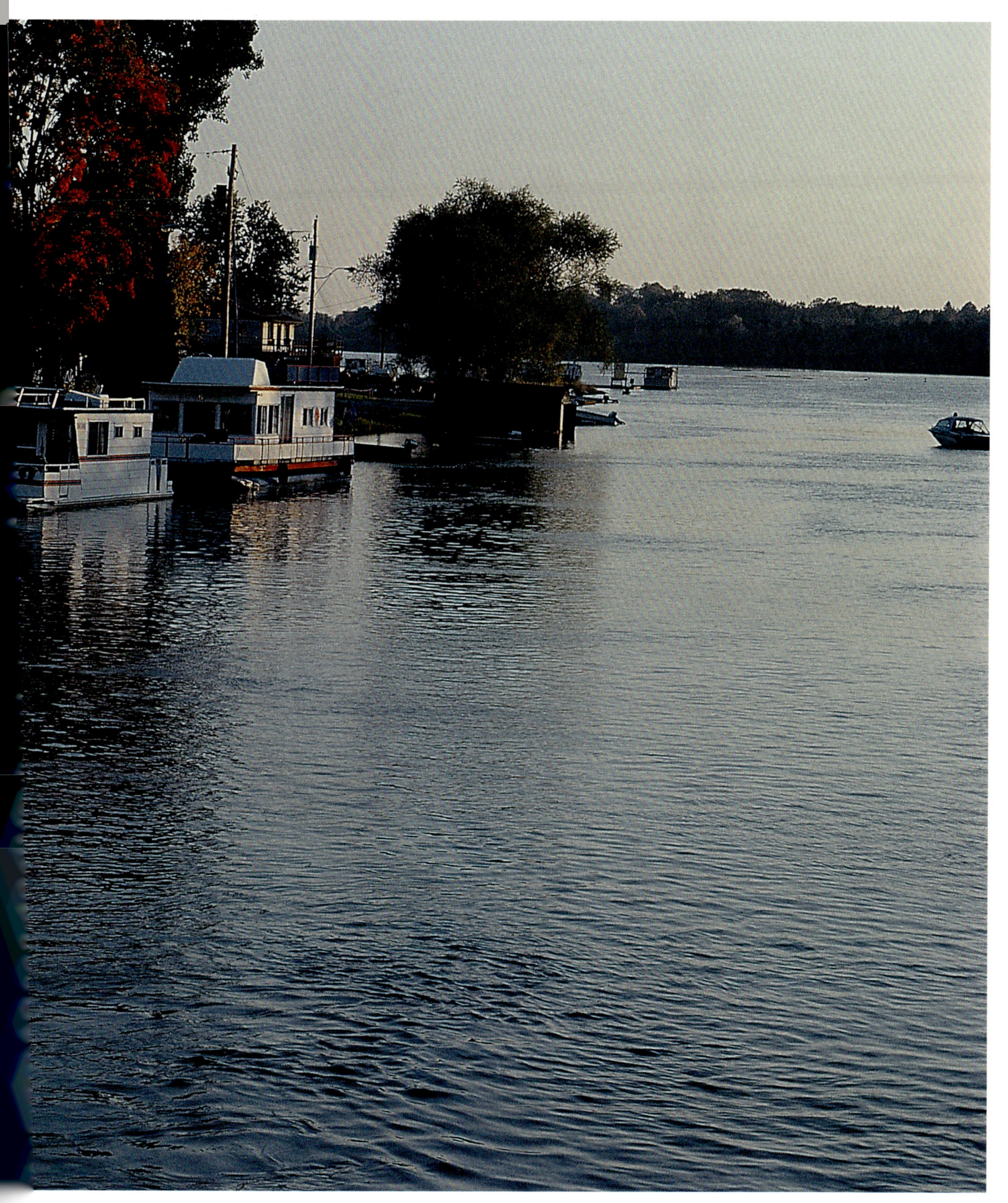

Just an hour's drive north of Toronto, Victoria County is one of the most accessible getaways. Anglers flock here each summer for record catches of bass, walleye, and muskie, and many lodges and resorts cater to vacationing families.

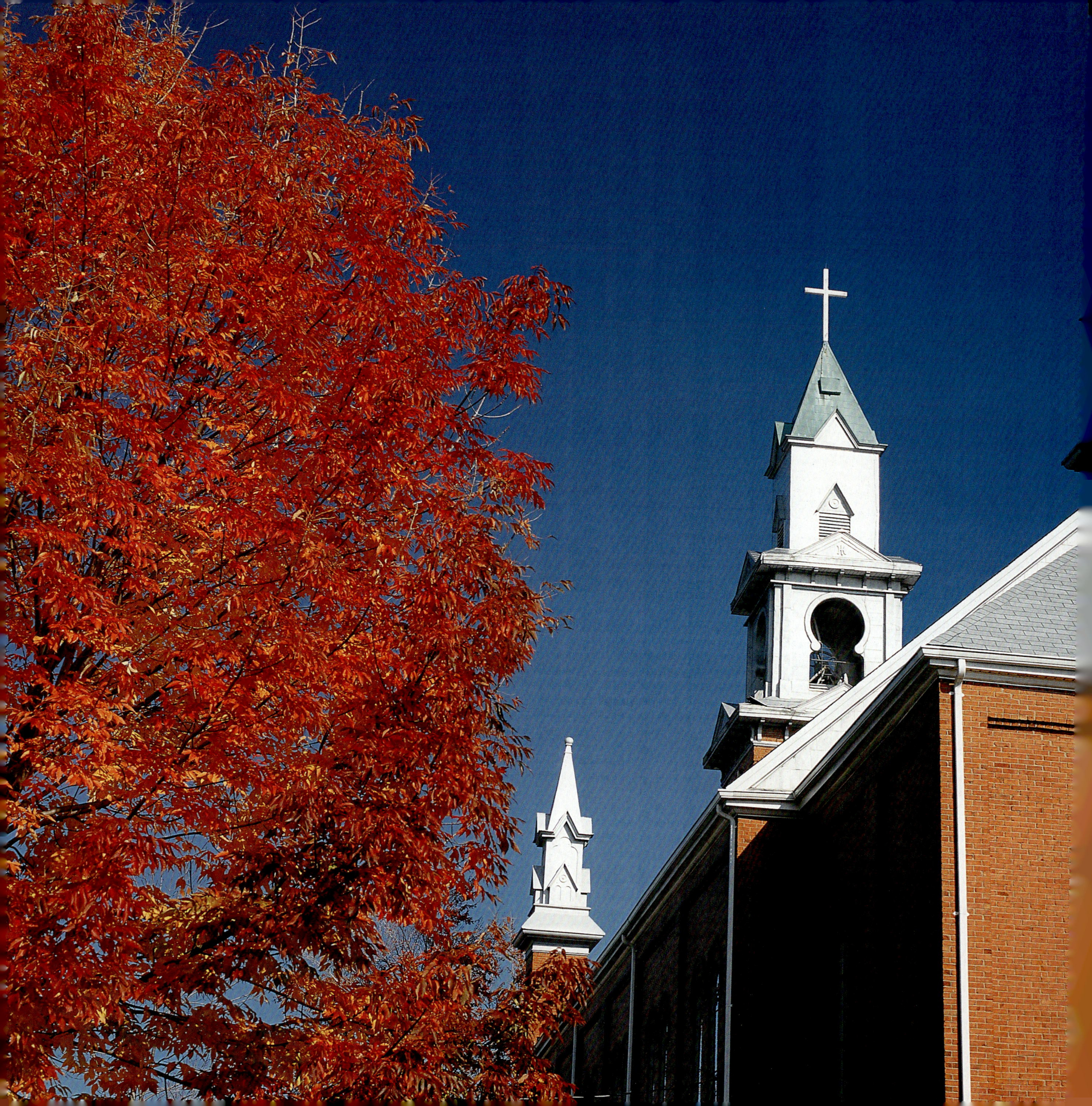

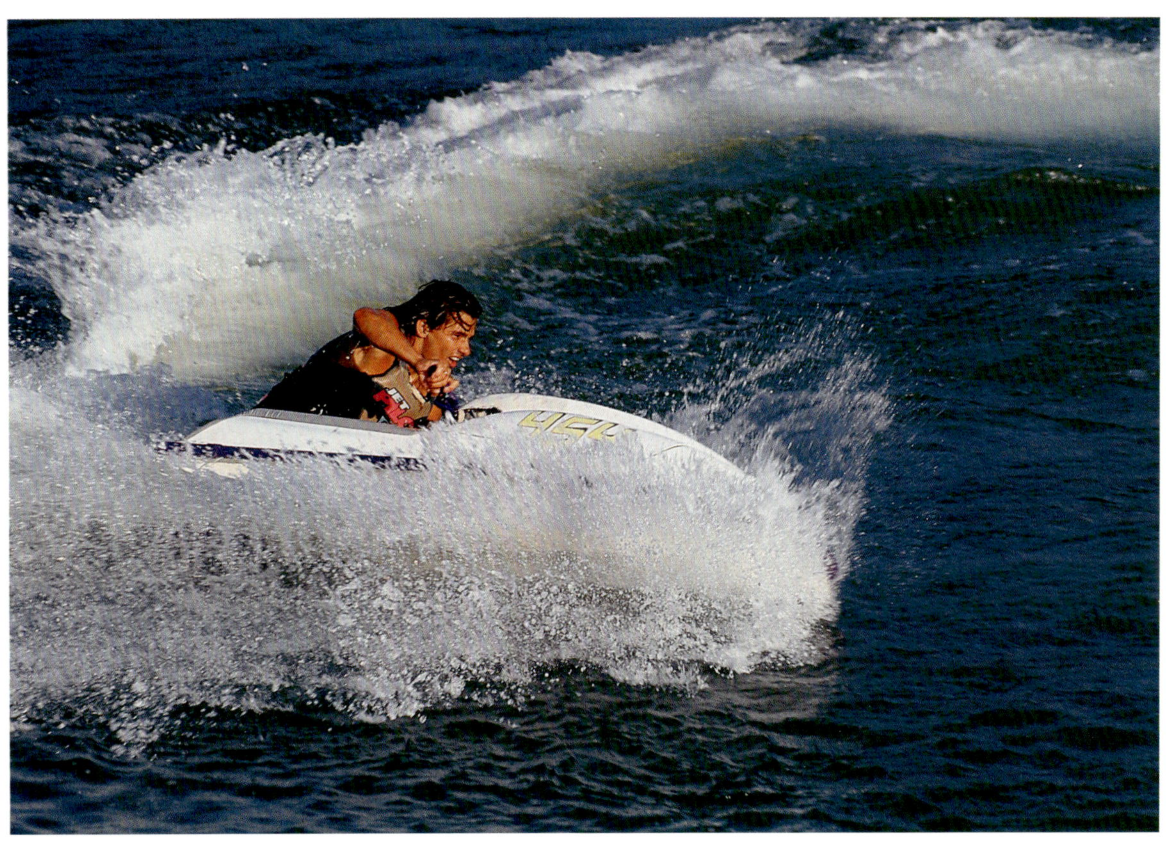

Once the domain of the solitary paddler, some of Ontario's waterways have attracted a more active crowd. Many of the smaller provincial parks offer access to motorboats and jet skis.

The Kawartha Lakes region was home to two of Canada's most famous settlers—Susanna Moodie, who recorded the hardships of emigration in *Roughing It in The Bush*, and her sister Catherine Parr Traill, whose *Backwoods of Canada* is one of the nation's best-known early botany guides.

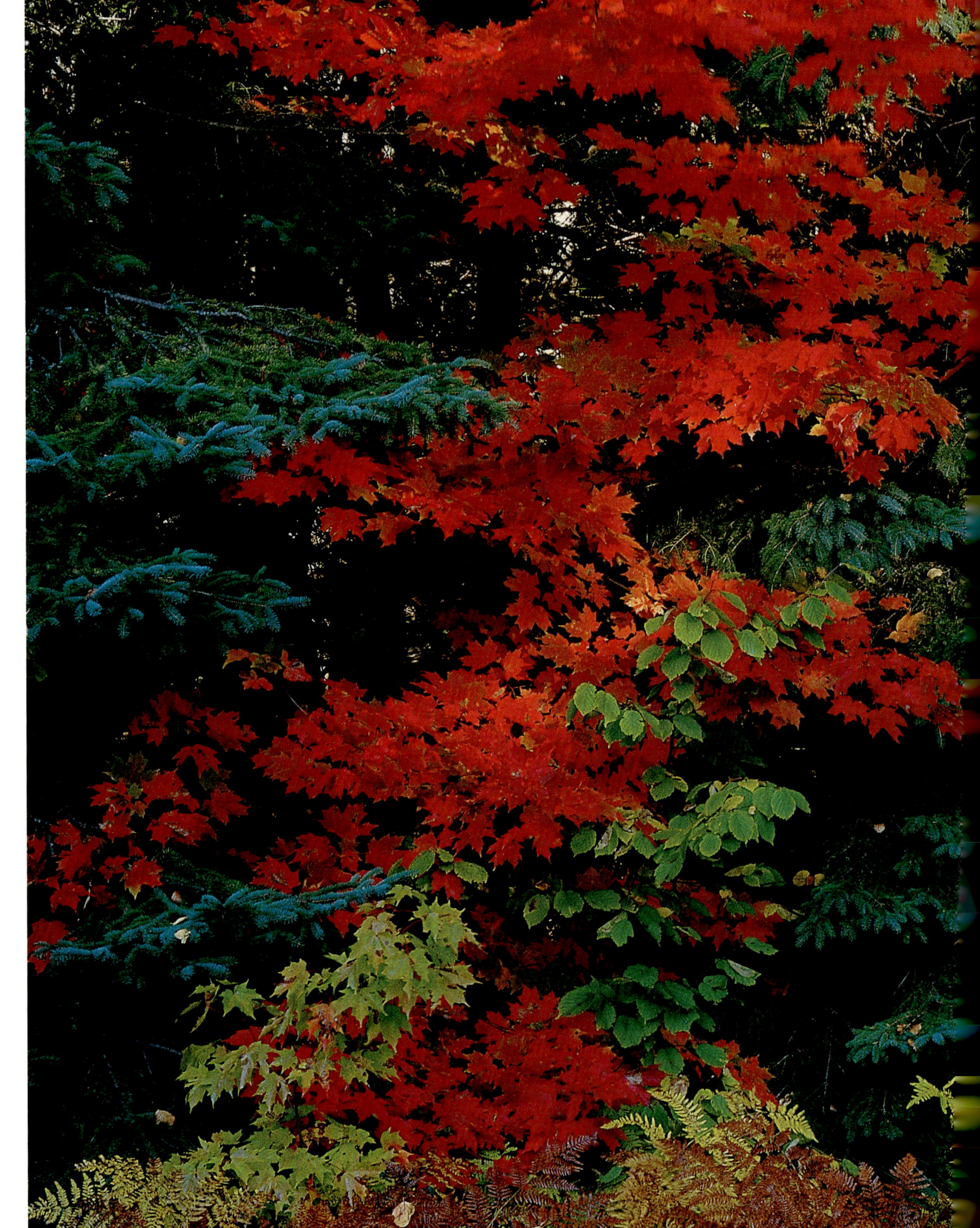

Fall colours brighten the hillsides along the Goulais River. A favourite destination for campers and paddlers, this region is protected by half a dozen parks, including Algoma Headwaters Provincial Park and Goulais River Waterway Park.

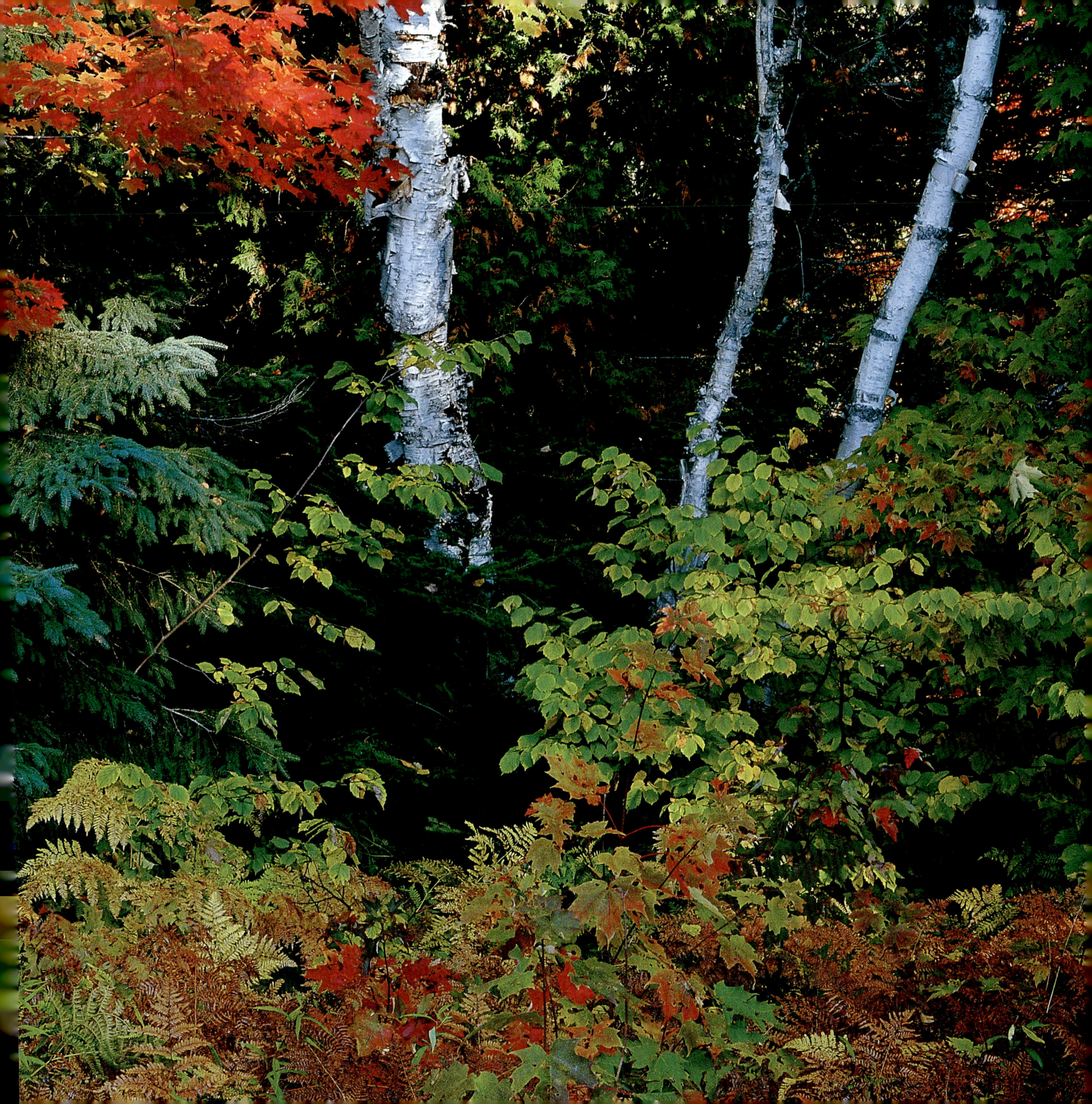

Photo Credits

Don Standfield/First Light 1, 3, 59

Mike Grandmaison 6–7, 8, 9, 10–11, 12, 20, 22–23, 24, 25, 26, 27, 30–31, 33, 38, 48–49, 50, 53, 54, 77, 82–83, 86–87, 94–95

John L. Bykerk/Lone Pine Photo 13, 16–17, 32, 78–79

Ron Smid 14, 15, 21, 28–29, 76, 80–81

Wayne Lynch 18, 42, 51, 64

Randy Romano/Turtle Pond Photography 19, 55, 68, 69

Clarence W. Norris/Lone Pine Photo 34, 36–37, 39, 65, 93

Bev McMullen/Lone Pine Photo 35, 40–41, 44–45, 46, 47, 71, 84, 85

Alan Sirulnikoff/First Light 43

John Bonner/Mach 2 Stock 52, 58, 75

Ron Watts/First Light 56–57

T. Amsden/Mach 2 Stock 60, 62–63

Darwin Wiggett/First Light 61

Greg Locke/First Light 66–67

Wayne Sproul/Mach 2 Stock 70

Roy Morsch/First Light 72–73

Aubrey Lang 74

Chris Cheadle/First Light 88

Kristopher Walmsley/Mach 2 Stock 89

David Jones/Mach 2 Stock 90–91

Stan Kwasniowski/Mach 2 Stock 92

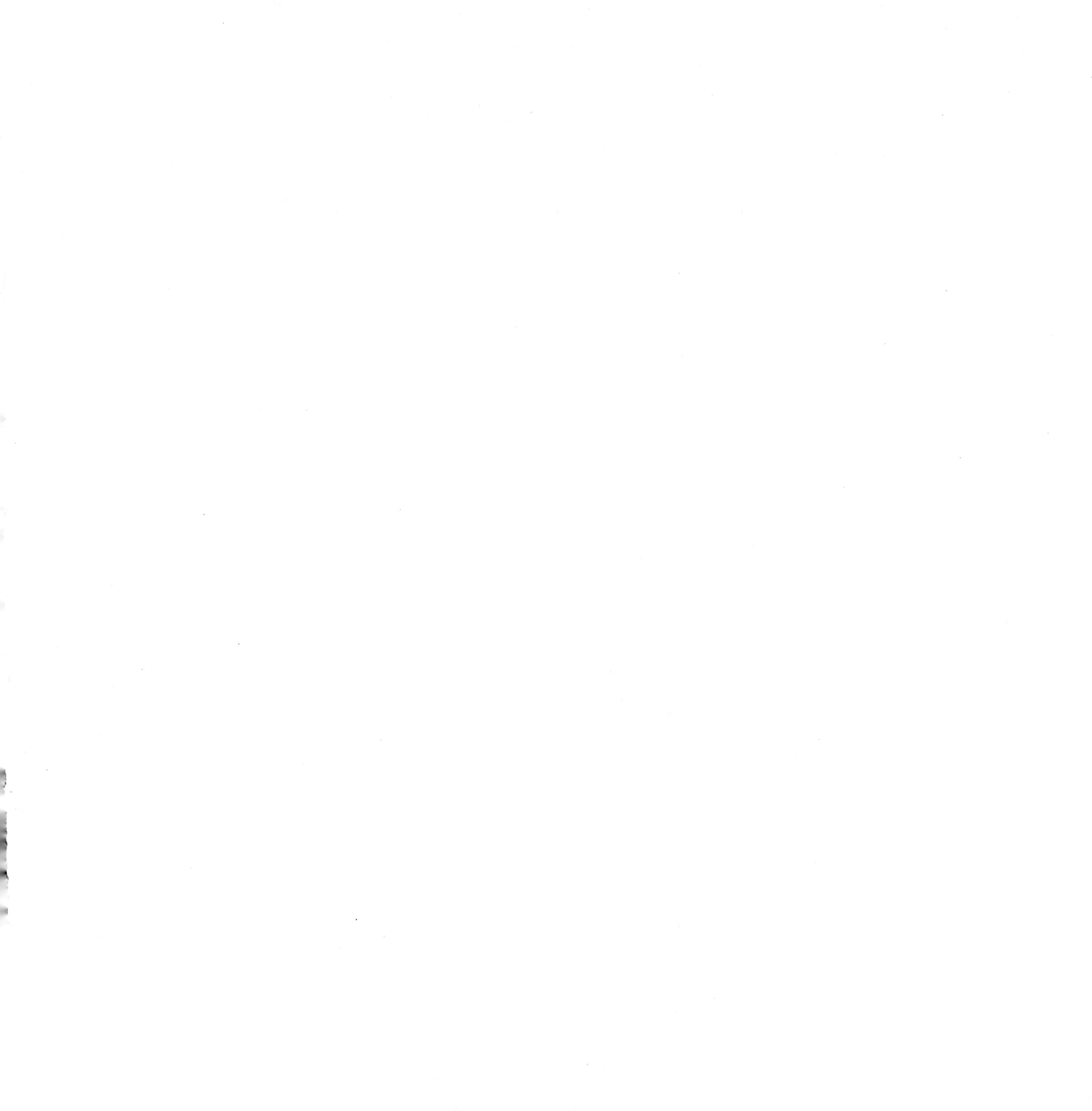